WICCA CRYSTAL MAGIC

Learn Wiccan Beliefs, Rituals & Magic, and How to Use Wiccan Spells Using Crystals & Mineral Stones

Lisa Miller

© Copyright 2020 by Lisa Miller

All rights reserved.

The material contained herein is presented with the intent of furnishing pertinent and relevant information and knowledge on the topic with the sole purpose of providing entertainment. The author should thus not be considered an expert on the topic in this material despite any claims to such expertise, first-hand knowledge and any other reasonable claim to specific knowledge on the material contained herein. The information presented in this work has been researched to ensure its reasonable accuracy and validity. Nevertheless, it is advisable to consult with a duly licensed professional in the area pertaining to this topic, or any other covered in this book, in order to ensure the quality and validity of the advice and/or techniques contained in this material.

This is a legally binding statement as deemed so by the Committee of Publishers Association and the American Bar Association in the United States. Any reproduction, transmission, copying or otherwise duplication of the material contained in this work are in violation of current copyright legislation. No physical or digital copies of this work, both total and partial, may not be done without the Publisher's express written consent. All additional rights are reserved by the publisher of this work.

The data, facts and description of events forthwith shall be considered as accurate unless the work is deemed to be a work of fiction. In any event, the Publisher is exempt of responsibility for any use of the information contained in the present work on the part of the user. The author and Publisher may not be deemed liable, under any circumstances, for the events resulting from the observance of the advice, tips, techniques and any other contents presented herein.

Given the informational and entertainment nature of the content presented in this work, there is no guarantee as to the quality and validity of the information. As such, the contents of this work are deemed as universal. No use of copyrighted material is used in this work. Any references to other trademarks are done so under fair use and by no means represent an endorsement of such trademarks or their holder.

TABLE OF CONTENTS

Introduction 1
Chapter 1 *Introducing Wicca* 2

    What Is Wicca? 2
    Thirteen Principles of Witchcraft 4
    History of Wicca 9
    What Wicca and Wiccans Are Not 11
    What Wiccans and Wicca Are 14
    Branches of Wicca 16
    Core Beliefs 20

Chapter 2 *Terms To Know* 22

    Absent Healing 22
    Acolyte 22
    Adept 22
    Akasha 22
    Akashic Records 23
    Altar 23
    Anima 23
    Amulet 23
    Animism 23
    Ankh 24
    An-shet 24
    Apprentice 24
    Aspects 24
    Asperger 24
    Astral Body 25
    Astral Plane 25
    Astral Projection 25
    Astrology 26
    Athame 26
    Attunement 26
    Aura 26
    Avatar 27
    Balefire 27
    Bane 27
    Banish 27
    Besom 27
    Between the Worlds 28
    Bi-Location 28

Binding	28
Blast	28
Black Magic	28
Black Moon	29
Blessed Be	29
Blood of the Moon	29
Bolline	29
Book of Shadows	29
Burning Times	30
Cakes and Ales	30
Candles	30
Cardinal Points	30
Cape	31
Cauldron	31
Censer	31
Centering	31
Chakra	32
Chalice	32
Channeling	32
Chanting	32
Charge of the Goddess	33
Charge	33
Charms	33
Circle	33
Clairvoyance	33
Cleansing	34
Cone of Power	34
Conjuration	34
Consecrate	34
Corn Doll	34
Coven	35
Covenstead	35
Cowan	35
Crone	35
Crystal Elixir	35
Cross-Quarter Days	36
Crystal Ball	36
Curses	36
Dawning Down the Sun	36
Days of Power	36
Dedication	36
Degrees of Witchcraft	37

Deflection 37
Deity 37
Deosil 37
Divination 37
Dowsing 37
Drawing Down the Moon 38
Earth Power 38
Eke Name 38
Elder 38
Elements 38
Equinox 38
Esbat 39
Familiars 39
Five-Fold Kiss 39
Fluffy Bunny 39
Great Rite 39
Grimoire 39
Group Practitioner 40
Handfasting 40
High Priest or Priestess 40
Hiving Off 40
Incantation 40
Initiation 40
Intentions 40
Invoke 41
Lady and Lord 41
Left-Hand Path 41
Libation 41
Lunar Eclipse 41
Magical Alphabets 41
Magick 42
Maiden 42
Manifest 42
Merry Meet 42
Mother 42
Necromancy 42
Neophyte 43
Numerology 43
Occult 43
Omen 43
Pagan 43
Palm Reading 43

Pantheistic	44
Pantheon	44
Pendulum	44
Pentacle	44
Pentagram	44
Personal Power	45
Planes	45
Potion	45
Prana	45
Precognition	45
Projective Energy	45
Receptive Energy	46
Reincarnation	46
Right-Hand Path	46
Ritual	46
Rule of Three	46
Runes	47
Sabbats	47
Scourge	47
Scrying	47
Séance	47
Shadow Work	47
Sigils	48
Skyclad	48
Smudging	48
Solstice	48
Solar Eclipse	48
Solitary Practitioner	48
Spell	49
Spirits of the Stones	49
Spiritualism	49
Summerlands	49
Summoner	49
Talisman	49
Tarot Cards	50
The Craft	50
Transmutation	50
Triple Goddess	50
Undine	50
Vision Quest	50
Wand	51
Warding	51

Warlock 51
Wheel of the Year.. 51
White Magic 52
Wiccan Rede 52
Wiccaning 52
Widdershins 52
Witch... 52
Witchcraft 53
Witches Ladder 53
Witching Hour 53
Zodiac... 53

Chapter 3 *Wiccan Rites and Celebrations* 54

The Wheel of the Year.. 54
Wiccan Rites 57

Chapter 4 *Mesmerizing Magic* 59

Types of Witches... 59
Tasks to Get Started.. 61

Chapter 5 *Crystal Magic* 64

History of Crystal Magic 64
Commonly Used Crystals... 66
Crystal Systems 78
Preparations... 79
Creating Crystal Magic 87

Chapter 6 *Beyond What Glimmers* 91
Conclusion 94
Description 95

INTRODUCTION

Thanks for purchasing *Wicca Crystal Magic*. Hopefully, it will give you all the information you need to start practicing Wicca. It should also answer any questions you have about Wicca answered. Whatever your reasons for wanting to read this book, I invite you to read it with an open mind so that you can seriously consider all the possibilities of Wicca. People have treated Wicca as something darker and scarier than what it is, so I've made every attempt to clarify the misconceptions that are commonly held and to show that Wicca is a unique but beautiful religion that is open to all kinds of people. No matter who you are, you can have a place in Wicca.

This book will teach you the fundamental ideas of Wicca and Wiccan crystal magic. This book is perfect for beginners who know nothing or next to nothing, but it can also be useful for people who know about Wicca but want to learn some of the details that you don't usually find with a basic search. While there are plenty of resources online, this book is unique because it compiles all the information you need to get started on Wicca into one book in a clear, concise, and fun manner.

Without further ado, enjoy this book, and let Wicca fill your life with some magic. By the end of this book, you should have a better understanding of what being Wiccan entails, and you'll know how to start practicing Wicca if you are so inclined.

CHAPTER 1
Introducing Wicca

What Is Wicca?

For those of you who may be unfamiliar with Wicca, it helps to have a brief introduction into what Wicca means before starting on your journey to becoming Wicca or learning more about it. Many people misunderstand what it means to be a Wiccan, which means that they don't even consider that it might be a good religion for them before dismissing it. The erroneous views of Wiccans often are because people hate what they cannot understand. Too often, people do not try to understand Wicca, which leads to all the misleading stereotypes and beliefs about Wicca that permeate Western cultures. The more you learn about Wicca, the easier it will be to see that it is just like any other religion in that it promotes morality and community. All that's different is its belief system.

Wicca is the most predominant form of paganism in the United States, and it is prevalent across the world as well. People often use the word paganism to refer to ancient polytheistic religions, but it is much more than that. In fact, paganism refers to any religion that is not Abrahamic. Abrahamic religions include Christianity, Judaism, and Islam. Pagan religions include Druidism, Hinduism, and, of course, Wicca. People use paganism as a derogatory word that means uncivilized because that's how Abrahamic people viewed the ancient religions when they came in and dominated religiously. They saw cultures that endorsed human sacrifice as well as other sacrifices, and they viewed them as wrong and ignorant. Modern pagan religions like Wicca are in no way associated with human sacrifice, but the early judgments still linger.

Unfortunately, because of the wrong associations linked to Paganism, there has not been a lot of academic work about Pagan religions, which means it is hard to have exact statistics about how many Pagans are in the world and what their common behaviors are. While Wiccans might not mind being more private, it does make it hard for their religion to spread and hard for people to share truthful ideas about Wicca. In the 1990s, there were increased academic movements that studied pagan faiths, but the research is still relatively new and far from mainstream. The increasing information that is becoming available about witchcraft is blossoming with the internet. Yet, even then, it is shocking how limited the information is about Wicca and other forms of paganism.

Wicca is a form of paganism, but it is important to clarify that it is not representative of what all types of paganism believe. Paganism does not always include witchcraft, but Wicca does include witchcraft. Wicca is its own religion that outsiders need to treat as such. Just because other pagan religions support immoral things or evil (though most don't) doesn't mean that Wicca also supports those things. Thus, it's essential to be aware of what religions really are before making snap judgments about them.

Wicca is a religion that commonly emphasizes two deities— the God and the Goddess. These deities have different aspects, which means that they take on various forms. Some versions of Wicca can have additional gods and be pantheistic, but that all depends on how you choose to practice and what you want to emphasize in your practice. Don't worry too much about that right now. To start, you can focus on the broad brushstrokes of Wicca. You can learn more about the details later.

Wicca centers itself around the moon cycles, which are called Esbats and are related to the Goddess. It also focuses on the sun cycles, which are related to the God and mark the Sabbats, which are the eight main festivals of Wicca. The celestial bodies, therefore, are essential to Wiccans because they represent the times when Wiccans are most potent, and they dictate when and how Wiccans practice their religion. Wiccans often strive to align their rituals with the cycles of the moon and the sun. By doing this, they form a link between the celestial and the natural. This link is a vital connection for any Wiccan to make.

The natural is one of the most critical parts of Wicca. Many Wiccan beliefs are rooted in maintaining harmony between Wiccans and the nature that surrounds them. Wiccans believe that everything in life has an energy and that even non-living things are essential because of the energy that they contain. Thus, utilizing entities like crystals and herbs can help Wiccans with their magic by providing energy and unique properties. To be a good Wiccan, you have to learn to respect the Earth and wisely use everything that is on it. Finding that harmony between what surrounds you and what is inside you is one of the most rewarding parts of Wicca.

While Wicca is one religion, there are many ways that you can practice it. Wiccans commonly use several branches, and some methods fall outside of the mainstream branches. Thus, it can be hard to pinpoint what Wicca is. Several words are often associated with Wicca— witchcraft, esotericism, occult, new age, polytheistic, magical. Because Wicca means so many things to many people, these words are just the start of all the things that Wicca can represent to its practitioners. When you are Wiccan, there is only so much you can learn from a book. The true meaning of Wicca becomes more apparent when you practice it and learn what it means to you.

Wicca is a unique religion that draws inspiration from several cultures. It is a relatively new religion, but its roots are ancient, and it strives to bring practices that have been deemed scientifically as "superstitious" or "mythical" back into fashion. The magic that Wicca practices isn't the kind that you know of magicians or from pop culture. Instead, it's magic that emphasizes the power of your mind to control your relationship with the world around you. Magic is real, but that doesn't mean it looks like how you think it should. Wicca is more than just a religion or witchcraft is a culmination of the two, and it is a beautiful spiritual force.

Thirteen Principles of Witchcraft

Thirteen principles drive Wiccan witchcraft among several Wiccan groups. While these beliefs can vary based on your branch of Wicca, they are seen as necessary in most branches or shape the foundation of most Wiccan religions. While no one thing is Wicca, these principles were created in 1974 to try to unify some of the Wiccan beliefs, and the Council made these laws of American Witches. You do not have to follow all of these based on how you practice, but they can give a good idea of what beliefs Wiccans find most important. They follow these rules along with the Wiccan Rede, which is that they should not harm others.

1. The seasons dictated by the moon distinguish Wiccans practice rituals and spells that help them become more aligned with the natural forces that drive life and these forces. The Wiccan holidays fall at the seasonal quarters and cross quarters. Everything that a Wiccan does centers around these forces, and they should drive themselves to channel their energy to reflect the forces around them and to celebrate the power that comes with those forces. The more Wiccans can be aware of the natural energies that surround them, the better able they will be to do spells and create more potent magic.

2. Wiccans recognize that they have a responsibility for the well-being of the environment because of their increased knowledge and love of nature. They strive to find balance with nature and protect it whenever they can. Wiccans do not want to harm the Earth. They want to help heal it and let it evolve as it needs to. They are not to neglect the sanctity of the Earth or anything on it because all things have energies that witches need to consider before doing anything. The health of Earth is vital to the health of the people on it, so it cannot be ignored by Wiccans.

3. Wiccans acknowledge that they have greater power than other people on Earth. They accept that some people will consider this power to be supernatural, but to Wiccans, this power is not supernatural. It is inherent within nature, and they have channeled it in their practices. They believe that anyone can bring magic into the world, but not everyone chooses to do so. The energies needed for magic are at each person's fingertips, and the joy of Wicca is knowing how to harness that power through the wisdom that has witches pass down through Wiccans via covens and oral histories.

4. Wiccans also embrace the polarity of the universe. There is a balance between the masculine and the feminine, and this balance gives Wiccans more power when they acknowledge it. Wiccans can be more creative when they manifest the

polarity of the universe. Interaction between the masculine and the feminine embrace this polarity and allow for more significant witchcraft. Neither masculinity nor femininity is superior to the other, which is one of the ways that Wicca promotes equality among people rather than trying to divide people. Wiccans should embrace both polarities for ideal results. This tenet also encourages the use of sex for not only a source of energy but a manner for obtaining pleasure and a symbol for life being personified.

5. Wiccans do not prioritize one world over the other. They recognize that there are both inner and outer worlds that include the unconscious. The various planes are not to be deemed as more important than one another because they are all paramount in the well-being of a Wiccan. The ability to create communication between the dimensions is the heart of magic and other spiritual encounters that are driven by the Wiccan religion. Allowing the other planes to exist and paying attention to them allows Wiccans to do things that other humans cannot do because they close their minds off to spiritual ideas and ignore the other planes that they cannot see.

6. Wiccans are against any hierarchy that creates authoritarian behavior, but they do honor people who are more advanced in Wicca and who pass on the traditions and keep it alive. Wiccans respect those who came before, but they can see beyond the hierarchy when they need and embrace individuality. Wicca is not like becoming a certain person. It is a way to practice one's uniqueness within a group setting. Thus, the insight of the elders should be valued, but it should not be the sole information that practitioners use to make their decisions.

7. Wiccans view knowledge, their religion, and magick as enmeshed. These three properties are a part of life, and Wiccans must incorporate all three into their behaviors. The art of witchcraft is a worldview that Wiccans share, and people cannot dissect this art while remaining Wiccan. Wicca is practiced in diverse ways, but both witchcraft and religion and the wisdom that go into them are linked in ways

that make them inseparable. Learn as much as you can about these three areas and look at them holistically to embrace the teachings of Wicca.

8. Wiccans believe that just because you use the title "witch" does not mean that you are a witch, nor does your family line alone make you a witch. It doesn't matter if you call yourself a witch or are in a family that has had generations of witches. Even those who are of the highest degrees of witchcraft are not witches if they do not embrace the energies around them. Wiccan witches must learn to balance all the energies and use them for functional purposes. To be a true witch requires control. Wiccans have learned how to control the forces within and without themselves, and they can do so with wisdom and morality.

9. Wiccans have faith in their abilities to learn about the universe and to give meaning to it through their craft. They believe that by doing magic and practicing their religion that they will have a better consciousness about commonly unknown things. They will become aware of parts of the universe that the average person never becomes aware of. This awareness will lead to fulfillment in the Wiccan's life, but this awareness is never finite. There are always more opportunities to raise awareness about the world and to become wiser. There will never be a day when a Wiccan is too smart or has a consciousness about everything. Being on Earth means that Wiccans have something left to learn.

10. Wiccans only feel resentment towards other religions such as Christianity because of those religions claiming that they are the only religions that will provide salvation and good things. Wiccans do not like the view that there is just one way to find personal solace and freedom. Unfortunately, many prevalent religions in the west preach that their way is the only way, which is discordant with Wiccan philosophy. Wiccans do not hate Christian religion in and of itself, so they do not claim to be the only way, and they do not try to prevent people from practicing their religions or look down upon those people for having different religions.

11. Wiccans in America have determined that they do not need to worry about the history of witchcraft or the origins of specific terms because those ideas do not help them move forward. They instead want to focus on the now and what the future will bring for Wiccans. Debating about what once was is a waste of time and energy because it will not bring harmony into their lives. Instead, Wiccans choose to focus on things that will bring them inner and outer peace presently. The past contains lots of good information, but you shouldn't treat the past with bitterness and over-attention because that will do you no good.

12. Wiccans do not believe that there is absolute evil, nor do they accept embracing this evil and using it in acts of witchcraft. Accordingly, they do not believe in Satan, and they indeed do not worship him. They acknowledge the right of others to worship the devil if that is what they think is right, but that can never be a Wiccan practice. Wiccans do not want to harm others in their practices. They are okay with witches practicing to get personal gain, but that personal gain can not be the expense of other people. Wiccans follow the Wiccan Rede, which is a law that insists that they don't hurt other people.

13. Wiccans believe that they should use nature to find fulfillment and to search for things that will give them health and well-being. They believe that all that they need to better themselves is surrounding them. All they need to do is focus their energies and find ways to balance themselves and their energies with the ones that are in nature. Wicca is a matter of finding harmony, which will promote the inner and outer tranquility that Wiccans strive to achieve. The universe has so much to offer, but most people do not embrace what they cannot see, so they miss out on many skills and acts that could make them feel more connected to their surroundings and themselves.

While the Council of American witches does not exist anymore, there are many sects of American Wiccans and witches that still use these fundamental doctrines to guide their practices. Further, many Wiccans across the world have similar tenets even if branches of Wicca have not worded them as such. Thus, these thirteen principles, whether you choose to use them or not, give you a better idea of what Wicca is as a whole and the general parameters that Wiccans follow.

History of Wicca

Wicca is a religion that you can predominantly find in the Western world. While Wicca has roots in the Celtic world and with other pre-Christian religions, Wicca was more heavily motivated by Victorian influences. During Victorian times, people would create societies in which they would practice magic in secret. At that time, witchcraft was criminal, but these groups persevered nevertheless and passed on their writings to the next generation. While it would be years before Wicca became fully formed, the writings and work of the Victorians would fuel the witches who would come years later. Thinkers like Margaret Murray, the "Grandmother of Wicca," who worked in the 1920s, and Aleister Crowley, who started occult work in 1914, were essential figures who predated the emergence of modern Wicca but were nevertheless influential in its creation.

There are forms of Wicca that came before, but the founder of modern is considered by Wiccans to be Gerald Brosseau Gardner. Gardner lived in Asia for a spell as a British civil servant, and he began to discover new things about himself and the world while he was in Asia. During his time in Asia, Gardner started to study the occult, which led to him organizing a religion around the information he unveiled. Much of what he learned was from sources like Aleister Crowley, a significant name in the world of the occult who was a witch during Victorian times. When he finished his service in Asia, Gardner returned to Britain just before WWII commenced. When he returned, he used esoteric knowledge from writings to begin interacting with occult groups that had already started in England. Doreen Valiente assisted Gardner in bringing his ideas to life and forming the Wiccan religion that we know today.

It was hard being Wiccan in early times. Until 1951, the United Kingdom still had laws that banned witchcraft, so it wasn't until those laws went away that Gardner was able to publish his seminal

1954 work, *Witchcraft Today*. This book was one of several that brought attention to Wicca and spread the ideas of the religion. At that time, he also started his own coven. The members of his new coven were central parts of the Wiccan development process, and they helped Gardner create a foundation for Wicca that would be better for more types of people.

Gardner himself did not call his religion Wicca, but the practice became called that because the people who practiced the religion were often titled, "the Wicca." It wasn't until after Gardner died in 1964 that Wicca became the title of the faith officially. The word is known to mean "wise people," which refers to the wisdom of other plans and spiritual realms that Wicca can reach through their practice of Wicca. When Gardner died, Wicca began to spread even more, and it reached far beyond Europe, where it had originated. Wicca blossomed in ways that Gardner probably didn't expect.

Throughout the 1960s, Wicca began to grow in popularity, and it spread to other countries like the United States. In the United States, Wicca, with its emphasis on nature and its forward-thinking views on femininity, echoed many of the movements already happening in the United States. For many people, it was a comfort during an incredibly turbulent decade. Wicca allowed people to engage in spiritual practices without having to be part of restrictive, well-established religions. Free-spirited people flocked to Wicca, and they began the Craft with eagerness. Wicca was something new and exciting, and it shattered the ideal of conformity that had been the status quo in the 1950s.

By the 1980s, Wicca had 50,000 practitioners in the world, mostly in Europe and the United States. The eighties brought new recognition to Wicca, and people began to see that it was a legitimate religion. In 1984, in the case of Dettmer v. Landon, the United States recognized that Wicca is classified as a religion. Before Dettmer v. Landon, authorities had said that Wicca was not a religion because it had occult activities; however, the case solidified that because it was common practice and followed all qualifications to be a religion that it had to be considered a religion. The decision to label Wicca an official religion was a victorious decision for witches everywhere, some of whom still didn't get the recognition they deserved, or they faced discrimination.

Wicca doesn't have a hierarchical structure like many religions, so while Gardner was important, he was not the only notable figure in the world of Wicca. Many Wiccans followed Gardner's teachings, but other people found unique ways to practice Wicca. As Wicca grew, it began to branch off into a new version of itself. Not all practitioners wanted to use Gardernarian practicers. Alexander Sanders was one of the earliest sects of Wicca to branch off. His practice eventually branched off into Dianic Wicca. Some of these Wiccans did not like the use of the word "witch," and they chose not to use that term even though they were still practicing witchcraft. Certain groups continued to practice in the nude, which was called traditionalist because practicing in the nude was practiced by witches before even Gardner was around. Others wore robes or just their regular clothes. Wiccans began practicing in whole new ways, but Gardner was still considered the founder of all things Wicca. Other leaders just took Gardner's ideas and tweaked them to match their needs as Wiccans. Thus, Wicca allows for considerable flexibility in its practices, and anyone can find a sect of Wicca that matches their needs and beliefs.

Presently, there are up to one and a half million Wiccans around the world. In the United States, there are 300,000 Wiccans, and Wiccans are the biggest group of neo-pagan faiths in the country. The breakdown of branches of Wiccans is less clear because there could be hundreds of types of Wiccans, which makes it hard to keep track of all the branches that have arisen since Gardner's time. Nevertheless, it is obvious that Wicca has become an important religion, and it is something that people continue to learn and join.

Wicca is the most prominent religion related to witchcraft, and it is a safe-haven for many people who are looking to belong and lay down spiritual roots. People practice it in many different ways, but no matter how you practice Wicca, it helps connect you to yourself and the world around you. Plus, it allows you to create some magic that will help you improve your life. What's not to like?

What Wicca and Wiccans Are Not

There are many erroneous views of what Wicca is out there. These views make Wicca seem like it is malevolent or scary. Unfortunately, in the 1980s, Satanic Panic arose, and it caused people to question all things that weren't Christian. They became certain that Satan was taking over society through occult behaviors and occultism. This led to incidents like the satanic ritual abuse, which were wrongful allegations against childcare centers that were false but sprung up in the eighties because of fears of the devil. Wicca is lumped in with Satanism, and people became fearful of it, but Wicca is not something that anyone should be scared of, and through debunking the myths around it, you'll be able to see that Wicca and Wiccans aren't weird and scary.

Wicca is not weird contrary to popular belief. Because Wiccans use magic, people often think that Wiccans are weird and mysterious, but that couldn't be farther from the truth. Wiccans aren't stranger than any other person. They have different beliefs that aren't often understood by Western culture, but their views are as reasonable as any other religion. Wiccans should not be judged by people who don't even realize what they are trying to do through their spiritual practices. Admittedly, there are some strange Wiccans, but they are not inherently odd because of their weirdness (nor is weirdness a bad thing)!

Wicca is not interchangeable with the witchcraft. While Wiccans practice witchcraft, there are lots of types of witchcraft that do not fall under the Wiccan branch, and some of those other practices are not religious like Wicca is. Other religions use witchcraft, but don't practice Wicca. Thus, Wiccans and witches aren't interchangeable words. You can call a Wiccan a witch (for most of the branches), but you cannot call all witches Wiccans. Some witches do not practice religion at all, and so to associate them with Wicca would not be like calling every Christian a Catholic.

Wicca is not devil worship. The link between Wicca and Satanism is entirely unfounded. Wicca is not an Abrahamic religion, which means that Wiccans don't even believe in the devil. In the Wiccan religion, there is no view of absolute evil, so no figure like Satan exists. Thus, any associations that have been made between Satan and Wiccans are not well-researched and are not accurately linked conclusions.

Further, people who call them Satanists *and* Wiccans may not understand what Wicca is either and are likely not real practitioners. If you ever hear that Wicca equals satanism, you are hearing the perpetuation of people vilifying what they don't know. In these cases, people make judgments without any understanding of what is factual. The more these judgments spread, the harder it is for people to understand Wicca.

Wicca is not evil. Just like Wicca isn't satanism, it also isn't evil. The Wiccan Rede ensures that Wiccan does not use their magic for evil. Evil acts do a Wiccan no good, so there's no reason to be afraid that a Wiccan is going to try to destroy the world or hurt other people. Wiccans respect the world inherently, so they will value all the energies that the Earth has rather than trying to hurt it. Wiccans prioritize acts that help themselves and the community without resorting to evil deeds. Morality is essential in Wicca, just as it is in other religions.

Wicca does not encourage harming others to better oneself. Again, the Wiccan Rede prohibits Wiccans from hurting others to benefit themselves. Of course, that doesn't mean that a Wiccan will never use their magic for immoral purposes, but when they do harmful acts, they *are* breaking the values that Wicca holds dear. Wicca is all about creating positive forces and allowing the bad ones to be improved, so to harm others is to harm the mission of creating balance. When you harm others, you break the balance and compromise the well-being of your spiritual self.

Wicca is not an ancient religion. While Wicca has ancient roots, people created it in the twentieth century, so it is not ancient in its practices. It borrows a lot from ancient and Victorian times, but it has embraced modern principles. Accordingly, it does not encourage some more uncivilized behaviors like human sacrifice. Further, it reflects current cultures in ways that older religions don't because it was born with modern challenges and beliefs in mind. Thus, it furthers ideas such as feminism and environmentalism.

Wicca is not a "fake" religion. Governments have recognized it throughout the world as a valid religion rather than one that has been fabricated. Let me emphasize: Wicca is real, and it is legitimate, so do not doubt that even if you don't want to take part in it.

Wiccans don't make animal sacrifices. They respect the energies of animals, and they don't need to kill them in rituals. There may be rare Wiccans who work outside of regular Wiccan circles who use such practices, but an animal (or especially human) sacrifice is not encouraged. It does not help Wiccans balance their power.

Wiccans aren't hypersexual. While Wiccans may be more sexually open and are welcoming of all types of people, that does not mean that Wiccans like to have orgies. Being incredibly sexual isn't inherently sexual. Some Wiccans do practice naked, but even then, their nudity is a way of doing better magic and worshipping rather than something sexual in nature.

Wiccans practice magic, but they aren't like the witches you see in pop culture phenomena like *Sabrina the Teenage Witch* or *Harry Potter*. Witches can point at something and have sparks zap out of their fingers. They can't have one thought and change a person into a zoo animal. Witches do have power, but their influence is less glamorous than it appears in movies and other pop culture.

Wiccans are much more than many people give them credit for being. They are not all the same, and Wiccans are free to take some liberties with their practices because Wicca is not as rigid as many other religions, which is why it is so appealing to those who practice it.

What Wiccans and Wicca Are

More important than what Wicca isn't and who Wiccans aren't is what Wicca is and who Wiccans aren't. It is the things that define Wicca and Wiccans that make it stand out from all else.

Wicca is inviting. One of the best parts of Wicca is that it is open to people of all genders, races, and sexualities. No matter who you are, there is a place in the Wiccan community for you. Wicca allows you to be yourself within a community of people who may not be accepted elsewhere. Witchcraft has long been something that is done for outsiders, and Wicca is a religion that continues that practice while adding additional spiritual values that help guide people and give them structure. Wicca does not close its doors to people who are unaccepted elsewhere. It is open to all who want to live by its tenets.

Wicca is driven by good. At its core, it wants to create a world and a self that it is better. Wicca wants to follow the right-hand path. It wants to further the goodness of the world because that is what will lead to spiritual health. In Wicca, no one benefits from doing bad. Bad deeds may fulfill temporary wants, but they will not be good for a person in the long run. Wiccans know that following the Wiccan Rede is the wise thing to do, and they know that while their magic gives them power, it must be used responsibly or their bad deeds will come back upon them three times over.

Wicca is magical. Wicca embraces spells, incantations, divining, and so much more. It uses magic as part of its rituals, so when you are Wiccan, magic is automatically a part of your daily life. It becomes one of the most important facets of yourself, and the magic helps you deepen your faith. With magic, you can expand your abilities, and those abilities allow you to better serve your coven. They show you the good in the world, and they give you the promise of balance.

Wicca is a community. Wicca allows you to connect with likeminded people who also want to create magic. It gives you something bigger to believe in, and it allows you to see the world beyond yourself. Wiccans can find groups that welcome them and make them feel safe. While you don't need to interact with other Wiccans, communication with people who share your faith is incredibly rewarding and it helps you grow as a person. When you can share spiritual experiences, you have more power, and you have a group of people you know will always support you and be there to guide you.

Wiccans are individuals, and they love to use this individuality in their religion. They are unique people even when they are a part of a coven. They make their own decisions and they value nonconformity. The Wiccan faith gives them guidelines, but it also gives them plenty of chances to be themselves and to embrace what makes them special. Wiccans are diverse, and that's what makes the Wiccan community so wonderful. No two Wiccans look the same; yet, they are just as welcome in the Wiccan community. Wiccans are boldy themselves, and that's pretty admirable.

Branches of Wicca

There are several branches of Wicca that can be found across the world. While the distinctions aren't all that important because of how flexible Wicca is and how it can be personalized to your needs, it may help to find a branch that appeals to you and that best meets your individual needs. This list of branches is not exhaustive, but it gives you a good idea of what kind of Wiccans are out there. Likely, there are hundreds of branches of Wicca that can be found. Therefore, there is a group for everyone. Don't feel a need to label yourself any particular way when you first get started. It can take some time before you realize what you want from your experience with Wicca. Let your process happen organically rather than trying to force anything.

Alexandrian

The Alexandrian Wiccans tend to be less restrictive and allow members greater liberty. This group was formed by Alexander Sanders with the help of Maxine, his wife. This group is very closely related to the Gardnerian group, but they are allowed more freedom with worshipping deities outside of the traditional Wiccan ones, and they have more options when it comes to the rituals. Alexandrians, for example, encourage followers to work in the nude because being naked is related to freedom, but they do not have to.

In this tradition, they still use two deities, but they primarily use the aspects of the Horned God and the Mother Goddess as the primary forms of the deities. This practice can be found across the world, and it is one of the more common traditions of Wicca. It is still fairly traditional even though it is less traditional than Gardnerian Wicca. Thus, this type of Wicca is perfect for anyone who likes Gardnerian Wicca but wants less rigidity in how they practice.

Caledonii

Caledonii Wiccans practice their Wicca based on the religious origins of tribes in Scotland that were called the Caledonii by the Romans. This is a Celtic inspired religion that is part of Caledonii, but it is a subgroup. The Caledonii believe in being welcoming to people and embracing diversity. There are three main branches of the Caledonia Grande Tradition: Caledonii Druidic Order, Celtic Wicca, and Caledonii Federation. There are also more minor branches such as the Culdee Church of Celtic Christianity. All these religions have Caledonia roots, but they are not all Wiccan, so keep that in mind as you do more research.

Celtic

Celtic Wiccans incorporate Celtic traditions into their worship. Celtic people were originally found in areas such as the United Kingdom, Ireland, and France before the Christians took over. The Celtic festivals are the basis for the festivals that Wiccans in all branches celebrate today. The festivals have been renamed to better reflect Wiccan tradition, but for Celtic Wiccans, they use the old Celtic names. Celtic Wiccans also learn about Celtic mythology, which has additional gods and goddesses as well as stories of other beings such as the fae. Celtic Wiccans are very different from traditional Wiccans, but these groups are perfect for those who wish to celebrate both Celtic and Wiccan cultures.

Dianic

Dianic Wiccans are considered to be especially feminist witches. This tradition was created based on the works of an author, Zsuzsanna Budapest. The Dianic covens began in the United States in the 1970s, and it spread throughout the decade. Dianic covens emphasize the role of the Goddess and this version of Wicca is, therefore, monotheistic in many cases. They celebrate different versions of the Goddess, but all these versions are still just one deity. They also often only have women as members of the coven. Dianic groups make women feel safe gathering and practicing their witchcraft with men being there to enforce patriarchal patterns. Some Dianic witches have branched off from the all-female groups, and they encourage all genders to enter their groups, and they acknowledge the God as a secondary figure to the Goddess. Thus, in Dianic groups, the most important distinction is the worship of the goddess above all else.

Eclectic

Eclectic is probably the most common branch of Wicca, but it is hard to tell the exact numbers of who is doing what kind of Wicca. Eclectic Wicca describes all versions of Wicca that are less rigid and don't make followers go down a certain path. Eclectic Wiccans are free to determine which deities they want to worship and even what holidays they want to celebrate. They make their own traditions. Eclectic witchcraft can be done in solitary or in covens, depending on what the individual Wiccan wants. This version of Wicca gives you the most options to define your own faith. It can be helpful to start your journey out here as you figure out what you want to get out of Wicca and how you want to practice it.

Gardnerian

This branch of Wicca is the original branch, and it is named after Gerald Gardner. Because this branch steps back to the original group of Wiccans, they tend to emphasize traditional beliefs, and they are more inflexible when it comes to how they practice. They often do their work in the nude, and their covens are run by High Priestesses. The hierarchy of the coven is more profound in this tradition than it is in other traditions. Gardnerians also tend to be highly secretive, preferring to keep to themselves. While Gardnerian witches have to follow more rules and stay true to the origins of Wicca, this rigidity is helpful for some witches who need more structure.

In the Gardnerian branch of Wicca, there are three degrees of witchcraft. The first marks when someone has been dedicated and initiated into a coven. The second degree marks when a witch has moved beyond fundamental witchcraft and has grown into the coven. The third degree is when members rise in ranks through the coven and have leadership roles. A "fourth" degree is when members become the High Priest or High Priestess, which is the highest rank in a coven. When they are at the third-degree, practitioners may start their own coven to allow growth in the Wiccan faith.

Gardnerians tend to be more secretive than other branches, and they have intricate rituals that more modern branches don't always have. This sect of Wicca is found across the world, and it is popular because it is the original branch of Wicca. Though, many Wiccans like to have less structure in their practice of Wicca.

Georgian

George Patterson created his own branch of Wicca. He encouraged his followers to be unique and to embrace their own paths. Much of what he teaches follows Alexandrian principles, but Georgian Wicca is even more laid-back, so it allows more liberty with how you practice it. Patterson would tell followers to do what works and to not do what doesn't work. While Georgian is one of the significant branches of Wicca, it is quite eclectic, and it retains structure while also allowing lots of flexibility. Many practitioners like this style of Wicca because it remains an individualistic whole, still being an organized religion. In Georgian Wicca, you can and should be your unique self.

Hellenic

Hellenic Wiccans incorporate Greek beliefs into their Wicca. It is a merging of the traditional Wicca as well as the ancient Greek religion. Some of the Greek gods that Hellenic Wiccans include are Zeus, Poseidon, Hera, and Apollo, as well as others. The Greek pantheon is open to Hellenic Wiccans to worship and invoke in spells. If you are interested in Greek mythology, you might adore this version of Wicca!

Seax

Seax is a style of Wicca that encourages a more solitary approach to the religion. It was founded by Raymond Buckland, who was appalled when he saw corruption within covens. He didn't like the way the hierarchy could cause weird power dynamics that took away from the religion, so he started a branch of his own that would be fitting to people who wanted the option to practice Wicca by themselves. This practice often uses some Germanic deities such as Freya. Further, it uses runes more heavily than other sects of Wicca. Seax is the most individualistic group of Wiccans beyond those who don't organize in these groups at all.

Core Beliefs

Certain core beliefs drive Wiccans to act the way that they do. These core beliefs are the universal parts of the Wiccan religion, and they make Wiccan distinct from other pagan religions. These beliefs bond Wiccans everywhere with a shared interest in values and parts of the world that are as said to matter the most. If you are interested in or feel drawn to the following beliefs, Wicca may be an ideal path for you, and it may help you balance your physical and spiritual selves. Even if they don't appeal to you right now, if you give Wicca a try, you might be able to learn and grow into these beliefs.

Nature is an important part of the Wiccan belief system. As you know, the natural world is full of energy that Wiccans use to their advantage. Magic, of course, is another crucial part of Wicca. Magic is used to varying degrees by Wiccans, but it is always part of a Coven's rituals. Like any religion, Wicca has rituals that it uses to worship the gods and to spiritually grow. These rituals connect the Wiccan community.

Wiccans believe in balance. They think that through their practices they can promote the balance in all areas of themselves. They believe that there is much more than just the physical self and that a person is made up of many parts that balance their physical, emotional, and spiritual parts. They believe in psychic energies and the ability to foretell the future as well as shape it through spells.

The belief in the God and the Goddess as the two prominent deities is one of the most important beliefs of Wicca across all branches, and these are so important that you could write a book just on the deities! These deities represent polarity in the world as they are both masculine and feminine and sun and moon. Both deities have different aspects that are various forms that they take to represent various things.

Wiccans believe in these ideas and so much more that you'll learn throughout this book. At their core, Wiccans want to find tranquility in their lives, and they want to manage the chaos that comes from being alive. They can manage this chaos by worshipping the deities, practicing magic, respecting the earth and everything on it, and allowing themselves to remain balanced even in the face of chaos.

CHAPTER 2
Terms To Know

There are many terms that it helps to know before diving into Wicca more seriously. Whenever you need clarification on a term, you can check back to this list for reference. Don't feel like you have to memorize all of these terms right now (that would be overwhelming). Instead, familiarize yourself with them and build upon your knowledge of these terms as you start going deeper into Wicca.

Absent Healing

This is a method of transferring positive energy to a sick person, but in this process, the healer is not with the sick person when the healing commences. This kind of healing refers to both healing of the mind, the soul, or the body.

Acolyte

An acolyte is a person in a coven who is new to witchcraft. This term often refers to the lowest rank of a Wiccan. Acolytes have only started their journey, but they have plenty of room to grow and learn from elders of their coven so that they can rise through the ranks.

Adept

This term refers to a witch who is incredibly talented in a certain form of magic. Usually, this term is used to describe people who have been Wiccan for a long time and have practiced extensively. It can be used by witches who are not Wiccan as well, but it is primarily a Wiccan term.

Akasha

Akasha is the fifth element after water, air, fire, and earth. It represents spiritual energy that is present on the earth, and it is part of all the other elements. Thus, it is a special and all-consuming element that can be found anywhere you look if you make the effort to sense it.

Akashic Records

Akashic Records are the histories of people's past lives as well as tons of other knowledge. They are found within astral planes, so they cannot be seen without astral travel. Some practitioners also believe that these records are prophetic and have secrets about the future as well.

Altar

An altar is an important space for Wiccans. It is where artifacts for worship are kept, and it is a focal point for ritual, sacred practices. Altars can contain various elements, but you can find these in the homes of witches, and they are personalized based on the individual witch's expertise. Usually, they are built to be elevated, but they may also be found on the ground. Some items that may be found on an altar include chalices, cauldrons, or candles.

Anima

Anima is the feminine parts of a man that are kept within his psyche. In Wicca, the balance between masculine and feminine energies is important, making the religion one that values both the power of males and females, which is one of the most special elements of the religion.

Amulet

An amulet is often found as a piece of jewelry, and it is a charm that witches will keep with them for better luck and protection. This item is made by humans, and it can be made sacred by the witch who wears it or other witches.

Animism

Animism means that people give souls to inanimate things. Wiccans believe that everything has energies that they can channel and use for spells, which is why Wiccans have great respect for the natural world and everything on Earth. Those who agree with animism think that everything on earth has a unique spirit. Thus, even things like rocks have energies that need to be respected.

Ankh

Ankh refers to a cross that has a circle on the top. This cross is of Egyptian origin, but some Wiccans use it in their practices.

An-shet

An-shet is a word that is used by some to describe a wand. Use whatever terminology that you feel most comfortable with or that your coven encourages.

Apprentice

Apprentice is another term that is sometimes used to describe a beginner witch. The terminology that is used for a beginner will vary based on the other Wiccans that you associate with and the type of Wicca that you practice. Apprentices often get special attention from those with higher ranks and get hands-on help with their witchcraft.

Aspects

Aspects refer to the deities in their other forms or personas. The Goddess, for example, often takes on three forms— the maid, the mother, and the crone. Those three parts all make up the same deity, but they are used to represent different parts of the overarching deity. The three parts of the female deity represent the various stages of life that women go through.

Asperger

An asperger is a grouping of several herbs (or another object that can let water through) that have been brought together to use for purification. This can be used either before or after a ritual. Water is put through the asperger during the purification, and the water can be put on people or things.

Astral Body

An astral body is a person within, the spiritual part of you, who travels when you astral project. It is the psychic version of your body. It can't be seen in the physical plane, but you can see it and others can see it in the astral realm.

Astral Plane

An astral plane is also known as an astral realm or word. It is a plane of existence separate from the one that you physically exist in. You cannot see the astral plane when you go about your normal life. You cannot put the astral plane into your GPS and expect to get there. While it can be hard to get to an astral plane, especially when you first attempt to, it is not impossible. Many witches can get there with practice. The astral plane is appealing to witches and Wiccans because it allows people to have a consciousness that they cannot reach in the regular realm of existence. In the astral plane, you can push boundaries that your physical body normally prevents you from getting near, which is why the astral plane can allow you to accomplish greater things and get in touch with your spirituality.

Astral Projection

Astral projection is the process you use to reach the astral plane. It means that you can separate your astral body from your physical body and project yourself to new places. This is often also considered an out of body experience. This process opens up your eyes to new experiences, and it is one of the most exciting adventures you can go on. It's like traveling without having to leave the comfort of your home. It does take practice to learn how to do this skill, but it is a wonderful process that can help you see beyond the physical plane.

Astrology

Astrology is a metaphysical science that explores the meaning of the celestial bodies and how their alignments can help people channel their energies to create witchcraft and how those celestial bodies can predict the future. Astrology uses bodies, including the sun, the stars, and the moon, to determine what will happen and how people should act. The zodiac is one of the most common astrological ideas, and it used the alignment of the celestial bodies to assign birth charts that dictate how people behave. Some Wiccans pay special attention to astrology, and for all Wiccans, the cycle of the moon is important because it marks the major Wiccan festivals. Witches often align their spells to the phases of the moon to ensure they are using their power as well as they can be. You probably already know your astrological sign, but astrology is much more than just your zodiac sign and takes extensive study.

Athame

An athame is a double-edged dagger that usually has a black handle. It is a knife that is mostly used for rituals rather than for cutting things. When this dagger is put into a chalice, it represents the joining of masculine and feminine. The chalice represents the female energy while the athame represents the masculine because it is a phallic symbol. You can also use this tool to create circles for witchcraft.

Attunement

Attunement refers to any activity that aligns the inner parts of yourself. When you are attuned, you feel calmer and it is a harmonious state.

Aura

Aura refers to an energy that is invisible to many people but can be seen by Wiccans and other witches when they train themselves to see it. Auras are glows that form around people, and these glows reflect the personalities and vibes of the people who the auras surround. The aura will be made up of different colors in different locations around the person. The different areas of humans that the aura reflects are chakras.

Avatar

An avatar is a soul that has a higher status and returns to a body with a lower status to teach less advanced people. This can be seen in Christianity through Jesus, and it can be seen in Hinduism through Buddha, but it is also sometimes applied in Wiccan practices as well. This can also be referred to as a Bodhisattva.

Balefire

A balefire is fundamentally a bonfire that Wiccans use for their festivals. These fires are mostly used on the festivals of Yule, Midsummer, and Beltane, but they can also be used to help with magic on non-holidays and other holidays than the ones listed.

Bane

A bane is something that is evil and is a force that tries to destroy things. Banes will make your life more difficult. Something that is a bane can be banished by a coven or individual witches.

Banish

Banish means to send away bad energies or entities via magic. Wiccans sometimes must combat harmful forces by banishing them. Banishment can be done as a group or as individuals. Wiccans banish things by using banishing rituals, which can take a variety of forms.

Besom

A besom is a broomstick that is used for magic. Brooms in pop culture are often said to be something that witches ride. You should not try to fly on your brooms. You'll end up hurting yourself, but you can use brooms to brush away negative energy and clear away any bad luck. Many witches favor wooden brooms because they more closely look like a tree and are closer to nature, but whatever broom you have will do.

Between the Worlds

This is a concept related to the circle that Wiccans use in many rituals. It is the idea that when in the Wiccan Circle, you are between the physical and the spiritual worlds. Thus, you can associate with those who are in the spirit world.

Bi-Location

This is a term that means seeing a person physically at the same time that others see their astral body.

Binding

Binding is using magic to inhibit either a person or a thing. When you do a binding spell, you commonly use ropes or other objects that you can tie into knots. Binding often requires learning about different knots and their purposes. Mostly, this is used to prevent a person from either hurting themselves or hurting others.

Blast

To blast someone is to curse them.

Black Magic

Black magic is the kind of magic that Wiccans do not permit. It is magic that is used to harm other people or trick them. It is often called "the left-hand path," and it is a path of evil. The witches who practice black magic are selfish and evil. If you want to use black magic, which I hope you don't, Wicca is not for you. Further, black magic is dangerous, so practitioners who use it put themselves at risk.

Black Moon

A black moon refers to an extra new moon in a month. Sometimes, it can also mean that a full or new moon is missing in a month. The black moon is a time when Wiccans have more power, so it is a time when Wiccans tend to do more spells and rituals. As a powerful time for witches, black moons can be incredibly exciting.

Blessed Be

Blessed be is a multipurpose phrase that Wiccans can use to greet and say goodbye to one another. They may also use it as a response in rituals. It is meant to remind Wiccans that they are surrounded by sacred things. When they say it, Wiccans use the three-syllable pronunciation.

Blood of the Moon

Blood of the moon is a term used to describe when a female has the most power. Often, this time aligns with a woman's menstrual cycle, which is why they call it the blood of the moon. Some witches align their spells with their menstrual cycle to channel their energy. Sometimes, this is only used when the woman's menstruation happens on the full or new moon. Of course, this term only is relevant for witches that have a menstrual cycle.

Bolline

The bolline is a knife with a white handle that is used for cutting. It is often used for herbs and inscriptions. Most Wiccans do not use this knife when they are not in the Wiccan Circle.

Book of Shadows

A book of shadows falls under the umbrella of the term grimoire. In its essence, it is a witch's diary. Wiccans use these books to keep track of their spells and write down incantations, rituals, and recipes. They log their experiences and jot down information that they think is most important. A book of shadows guides a witch and allows them to look back on all the work they have done. Your Book of Shadows doesn't have to be anything fancy, but you can buy some really nice journals that would do the trick. While some witches follow the practice of burning books of burning or otherwise destroying books of shadows when other witches die, some switches pass their books down to their loved ones to guide them. Though, often, traditions are passed down orally. The book of shadows got its name from the burning times when witches had to practice in the shadows to avoid being persecuted.

Burning Times

This term is a reference to when witches were killed for practicing witchcraft. It specifically refers to when the Catholic church killed pagans for their beliefs during the Inquisition and Reformation. Witches were burned in some areas, but they were hanged in others. Witches do not face the persecution that they once did, fortunately, but burning times is a reminder of the bad that can happen when witches are unfairly vilified.

Cakes and Ales

This term refers to a meal that is had at the end of a Wiccan ritual. It is often shared with the gods and goddesses.

Candles

You probably are familiar with burning candles for the lovely smell that they can have, but they are so much more than that to Wiccans. Wiccans often use candles and wax in their rituals. Differently colored candles have unique meanings, and they are used for distinct rituals based on those meanings. Frequently, rituals are commenced and ended with lighting and blowing out the candle. The candles usually are consecrated by witches, and they can be made of herbs or symbols can be carved into them.

Cardinal Points

Cardinal points are the directions north, south, east, and west. Pointing things in different directions can have different meanings during a ritual. In some traditions, the north is represented by green candles. South is represented by red, east is represented by yellow, and the west is represented by blue. In any case, the cardinal points are used to draw the Wiccan Circle, which is made based on the cardinal points.

Cape

A cape is often used for witches to better use their power. These capes will often be embroidered with special symbols, and they were only worn in the presence of the deities. Wiccans take them off when they are outside of their sacred spaces. Not all Wiccan wear capes, but some may choose to do so.

Cauldron

A cauldron is one of the tools that most people already associate with witchcraft. Cauldrons are used for several purposes, and they are most often made of iron, but you can use a regular pot that you already have in your house if you'd rather. The point is to be able to make good spells and potions, so if you don't have money to spare, don't worry about what your cauldron looks like because the quality of your magic is more important than your equipment. Cauldrons often represent being well-fed, both physically and emotionally. They also are a symbol of the Goddess' womb. Thus, they are used for potions and scrying that ensure the well-being of Wiccans.

Censer

This is an incense burning container that can withstand heat. This is associated with the element of air because it is used to interact with the air via the smoke of the incense.

Centering

Centering is similar to meditation because it is the ability to transfer your consciousness from the physical self to the spiritual self. What that means is that when you center, you can channel your internal energy and escape the external forces that are destroying your energy. The more you practice centering, the easier it will become.

Chakra

Chakra are energy wheels that are found in various sections of your body. The seven primary chakras are root, third-eye, solar plexus, sacral, throat, heart, and crown. You need to find harmony between all these parts to stay mentally, physically, and spiritually balanced. The color red represents your root, which signifies the well-being of your physical body. Your third-eye is indigo, and it is correlated to the middle of your forehead and controls your intuition. Yellow is the color of your solar plexus and is linked to how you feel. Further, your sacral part is orange. Your throat is blue and represents spirituality. Your heart is green and this chakra is linked to astral projection. Finally, your crown is purple, and it is linked to your connection with the cosmos.

Chalice

A chalice is another ritual tool that looks like a goblet. It is commonly associated with the feminine energies. Further, it can be used to drink wine, water, or juice (or anything else really). It is often a consecrated, sacred item that is placed towards the west of your altar. It is used prominently in the Great Rite.

Channeling

Channeling is the act of using psychic powers to speak to a spirit, usually through another host. This term is also used to describe channeling energy, or focusing energy, to complete spells.

Chanting

Chanting is the repetition of certain words during your practice of Wicca. The repetition can be used to bring what you want into fruition. Many incantations will require you to do some chanting. Further, various rituals that you practice with a coven will require this as well. For beginners, chanting can make you feel silly, but once you get the hang of it, it will become an important part of your practice of Wicca.

Charge of the Goddess

The high priestess of a coven normally gives the Charge of the Goddess, which is the words of the Goddess given to her Wiccan "hidden children," who are her followers.

Charge

Charging often refers to crystals, and it is the act of putting energy into an object using magic. It can be done to accomplish several tasks such as luck or protection.

Charms

Charms are objects that have been given magical energy. They are an umbrella term for objects that have been charged, consecrated, or charmed with good energies that will help you accomplish specific tasks. They can be amulets, crystals, or talismans.

Circle

The Wiccan Circle, or more generally a witch's circle, is a sacred space that is created to celebrate, worship the deities, or to create magic. Covens often have certain ways that they will prepare their circles, which can vary greatly, but all circles are sacred spaces. The circle can be created simply by visualization, but it can also be marked with a sacred knife. For Wiccans, the circle is often seen as a transformative place that is between the spirit world and the physical world.

Clairvoyance

Clairvoyance is a psychic skill that allows people to be aware of future events. Not all clairvoyance will have the same level of clarity or the same perceptions of the future. Some clairvoyants won't even be able to tell the future, but instead, they will be able to know about past events that they weren't around for.

Cleansing

To cleanse something means to eliminate any bad energy that it contains. When something is being cleansed, the negativity will be banished from it to ensure nothing nasty lingers. Wiccans often do this daily to make sure that there aren't bad forces near them.

Cone of Power

The cone of power is an abstract concept because the cone can't typically be seen, but it is the power that one or multiple witches create as they are trying to complete a particular task.

Conjuration

Conjuration is using words to evoke a spirit. Many people find this act to be intimidating, but conjuring isn't like what you see in horror movies. If you do it the right way, it doesn't have to be wild and unpredictable. It can be under your control when you channel your energy correctly.

Consecrate

Consecrating something means to cleanse and then bless an object to not just banish the negative energies from it but to add sacred energy to it. Wiccans must be clearer about their purposes when they consecrate an object than when they cleanse it. A clear intention about what they want from the object helps clarify their purposes. Consecrated things have elevated value to Wiccans once they are consecrated.

Corn Doll

A corn doll is a small doll that is usually made to look like a human. Because corn used to refer to all grains in early times, the doll does not have to be made of corn, and it was originally made of agricultural goods to represent fertility. These dolls are still used in various Wiccan rituals, particularly in Europe.

Coven

A person's coven refers to the Wiccans that they worship and do their magic with. Basically, a coven is a witch's church, but covens are generally smaller than your average church. The maximum number of witches in a coven is usually fifteen, but many covens limit themselves to thirteen or less. Covens need at least three people. Not only does a coven do magic together, but they also will celebrate festivals together and are a community that bonds over their shared beliefs.

Covenstead

A covenstead is where witches come together and do their magic. It is their home base, and it is where the coven regularly meets.

Cowan

Cowan is a derogatory term that is used to describe people who are not witches. It is not a term that I would suggest you use because of its derogative nature, but you may hear it in Wiccan groups periodically.

Crone

A crone is one part of the familiar triple goddess archetype, meaning one part of a single deity. The crone is the old woman part of the triple goddess, and she represents wisdom and the end of life.

Crystal Elixir

Crystal elixirs are elixirs that have used crystals. To create these elixirs, you place crystals in water and other liquids, often with other herbs and items thrown in. The energy that the crystal adds to the elixir can be beneficial in witchcraft. These elixirs are often drunk and used for healing or improved magic.

Cross-Quarter Days

This term is what the Fire festivals, Samhain, Imbolc, Beltane, and Lamma, are called. They are four of the eight major festivals in the Wiccan religion.

Crystal Ball

A glass or crystal ball that you can use for scrying.

Curses

These are spells that put malevolence upon other people.

Dawning Down the Sun

Dawning down the sun means to invoke God into oneself. Witches can increase their powers through this ritual.

Days of Power

Days of power are the times when witches are at their most powerful. These days include your birthday, Blood of the Moon, anniversaries of being initiated, Sabbats, and miscellaneous astrological happenings.

Dedication

Dedication is a process that witches go through when they accept the Wiccan path and strive to reach an adept status someday. This process occurs before initiation, and it lasts for a year plus one day commonly, but the exact process may differ depending on your coven.

Degrees of Witchcraft

In witchcraft, witches will have different levels of skill, which are called degrees. The degrees that you must go through will depend on the coven, but generally, they are as follows: neophyte, middle stage, and full membership. The clergy is also held at a different level, a fourth-degree, in many Wiccan covens.

Deflection

This process generally uses a mirror to deflect evil forces away from you. When you deflect, you take bad energy and put it onto something else.

Deity

Deities refer to gods and goddesses who have supreme power. These beings are not human and have unique powers and properties. Wiccans celebrate multiple deities and often focus on the God and the Goddess as the two most prominent forces.

Deosil

Deosil means that, in a ritual, motions must be made in a clockwise manner. Many rituals will require you to act in this manner. It is commonly used in the northern hemisphere and represents good energies.

Divination

Divination is the process of obtaining knowledge about the future, present, or past. It often uses psychic abilities like clairvoyance, crystal balls, tarot cards, or scrying. It refers to all the methods you could use to get some knowledge that ordinary people would never have. While divination often uses tools, it doesn't have to. You can divine using simple things you have around the house.

Dowsing

Dowsing is the practice of using a pendulum, forks, or rods in magic to find a location. These tools can be used with a variety of methods.

Drawing Down the Moon

This practice means to invoke the Goddess into oneself. It is a way of channeling the divine and becoming more powerful.

Earth Power

Earth power refers to the energies that you can find in earthly objects like pants, rocks, and crystals. Wiccans believe that all these things have energies. Thus, they can be used for magical purposes.

Eke Name

This is a name that you have that is only used in divine spaces. It is secret to anyone but your fellow worshippers or the deities.

Elder

Elder is a title usually given to third-degree witches who are older than the others and commonly are known for being wise. Only some Wiccan groups have this distinction.

Elements

The five elements are part of many rituals. Some witches specialize in using certain elements, and they feel more akin to certain elements than others. The elements are fire, water, air, earth, and spirit, which make up the earth and everything that is on it. These elements can be used to increase the power of your spells because they tap into nature and allow you to focus on your intentions more easily.

Equinox

Equinoxes happen twice a year, and they are the time when the sun goes over the equator. They mark certain Wiccan holidays.

Esbat

Esbat is when witches gather, usually around the time of the full moon.

Familiars

Familiars are animals or other non-human spirits that guide witches. They allow witches to magnify their powers and better focus their energy. These familiars can be your pets or any creature that you feel helps you better your magic and focus your powers.

Five-Fold Kiss

The five-fold kiss is done before entering a ritual circle, and witches will kiss five spots: feet, knees, stomach, breasts, and lips. You do not have to do this ritual if you do not feel comfortable with it.

Fluffy Bunny

This idea is a term used to mock practitioners who are seen as being shallow in their practice of Wicca.

Great Rite

The Great Rite is a sexual ritual that uses sex to create more energy and focus the power of two witches. It is especially essential on the festival of Beltane as well as other special occasions.

Grimoire

A grimoire is a term that refers to written down spells or accounts of witchcraft. A Book of Shadows is a type of grimoire, but any book with magical properties in it can be a grimoire.

Group Practitioner

A group practitioner is a witch who does magic within a coven rather than alone. Wiccans are encouraged to be group practitioners and to join covens to celebrate their religious beliefs and practice white magic. For some people, the group element of Wicca is important.

Handfasting

Handfasting is the Wicca version of a marriage ceremony.

High Priest or Priestess

The high priest and priestesses are the leaders of their covens.

Hiving Off

Hiving off is when people leave one coven to start a new one and branch off from their original group. Hiving off allows the Wiccan religion to grow and expand without covens becoming too big.

Incantation

An incantation is a spell that uses words to craft your intentions and bring them to life. You've probably heard of incantations before, such as abracadabra. They can be as simple or as complex as you want them to be.

Initiation

Initiation is allowing new members to become part of a coven. During initiation, the person joining the coven will acknowledge that they want to join the group and reaffirm that they believe in what their new coven believes in. Several rituals take place during the initiation.

Intentions

Intentions are some of the most important parts of magic. Whenever you do magic, it is crucial to have an intention behind it, which is a clear idea of what you want to happen when you cast your spell.

Invoke

When you invoke in a ritual, you call upon the deities to give you energy and support.

Lady and Lord

Lady and Lord are ways that people sometimes refer to the God and the Goddess. These terms can also be used to show reverence for the High Priest or Priestess.

Left-Hand Path

The left-hand path refers to using black magic, and it is not a path that Wiccans are permitted to go on.

Libation

Libation is an offering of wine or water that you pour on the altar after you complete a ritual. You do this to show respect and gratitude to the God and the Goddess.

Lunar Eclipse

This occasion is a special occasion that celebrates the Goddess' aspects such as the crone.

Magical Alphabets

Some Wiccan traditions use magical alphabets in their rituals, spells, and books of shadows. Magical alphabets are basically just codes to keep your information secret. The need to keep this info secret isn't as great as it once was, but some Wiccans still use magical alphabets such as the Theban alphabet, which is a common magical alphabet.

Magick

Magick is a term often used by witches to separate witchcraft from stage magic. Aleister Crowley, sometimes known as Uncle A, was likely the one to add the K to magic. Many witches, including Wiccans, add the K when they do magic.

Maiden

Maiden, or maid, is the first part of the triple goddess, meaning that she is one part of the overall goddess. She represents youth.

Manifest

Manifestation is being able to channel your mental energy to make what you wish to come true a reality. Manifestation uses several methods, such as visualization, intentions, and even lucid dreams, which are dreams that you can consciously control.

Merry Meet

This is a phrase used to greet other Wiccans.

Mother

Mother is one of the parts of the triple goddess. She is the middle-aged part that represents fertility and motherhood.

Necromancy

Necromancy means dealing with dead people in your magic. Witches often try to deal with spirits and communicate with them for information. Necromancy is often scary for the new witch, but it doesn't have to be dark, and it can be incredibly rewarding.

Neophyte

A neophyte is someone who has just joined a coven and has not yet been initiated. Neophytes will have to take time to learn the craft before joining as a full member of the coven. A neophyte is called a wiclet in specific settings.

Numerology

Numerology is a method of divination that uses numbers and formulas to find answers. Each number corresponds to a letter from the alphabet, and this process is often used when you want to get a witch name or a name within your coven. Numerology is especially appealing to people who love to work with numbers, but even if you aren't a numbers person, it is manageable.

Occult

Occult is a word that means the study of the "covert secrets of the universe." It often explores supernatural elements of the world, but it also studies witchcraft and witches. The occult has long been misunderstood and is often viewed as scary, but it is not as terrifying as it may seem in horror films.

Omen

An omen is a sign that suggests that something might happen. It can either be a good omen or a bad one.

Pagan

Pagan refers to all religions that aren't Abrahamic. It includes Wicca, but it also includes many more religions that aren't necessarily associated with witchcraft.

Palm Reading

One form of divination is palm reading. Palm reading uses the lines and ridges of your hands to predict your future. It takes time to learn all the meanings for palm reading, but it is a rewarding craft.

Pantheistic

Wiccans are pantheistic, meaning that they see divine energy everywhere they go. Everything in life has that divine energy, and even non-living things are considered to be part of the divine.

Pantheon

A pantheon is a selection of deities that a particular religion accepts. Some religions have rigidly decided gods, but in some Wiccan groups, Wiccans are allowed to choose from the pantheon of the deities.

Pendulum

Pendulums are objects that are attached to ropes of chains, and they are then moved back and forth, and you can use them for dowsing.

Pentacle

The pentacle is one of the most important symbols in the Wiccan religion. It is a star with five points, and it represents the five elements— earth, air, fire, water, and spirit. Witches, including Wiccans, often have talismans and charms that have the pentacle on it, and they also use it for their rituals.

Pentagram

A pentagram, like a pentacle, is a star with five points, but in its history, it has taken on connotations that don't represent what Wicca stands for, which is why a pentacle is more commonly considered the primary Wiccan symbol. Pentagrams have become associated with Satanism, which makes pentagrams seem like something they are not.

Personal Power

Your personal power is the power that keeps your body running and allows it to do magic. It was given to you by the Goddess and the God through their own power. Everyone has their own kinds of powers and special abilities that other people don't have.

Planes

These are the various levels of existence. Some examples of the planes are: Physical, spiritual, etheric, astral, and mental. You can become more aware of these planes via magic.

Potion

A potion is a liquidy mix made with herbs and other magical ingredients. It is made to be part of various rituals.

Prana

All living things are part of the cosmic order, and that is prana, the energy of all that are culminating in a strong force.

Precognition

Precognition is the psychic ability to know what the future holds. Some people have a stronger sense of the future than others.

Projective Energy

Projective energy is the energy that sends things away from you. You can use this energy to get rid of negative forces by channeling positive ones. Your dominant hand is your projective hand. Thus, right-handed people use their right hands for projective energy while left-handed people use their left-hands for projective energy.

Receptive Energy

Receptive energy is pulling forces towards you. Many people use crystals to bring in good energy. Your non-dominant hand is your receptive hand, so if you are right-handed, your left hand is your receptive hand. If you are left-handed, your right hand is your receptive hand.

Reincarnation

Reincarnation is the belief that a person goes through multiple physical bodies. They are reborn to learn and become better souls. Each time people are reborn, they take on a new form based on what they need to advance and improve as beings; thus, people may go through multiple bodies, not even all of them human, throughout life.

Right-Hand Path

This path is the path of goodness, the Wiccan Rede, and white magic. It is using your magic for good rather than selfish and evil purposes that result in harming others.

Ritual

A ritual refers to any action that channels and concentrates your energy to accomplish one predetermined task. Rituals are repeated behaviors that follow the same patterns, and you can have rituals within religious contexts as well outside of religion.

Rule of Three

The rule of three is an important Wiccan belief. While not all Wiccans believe it, many do. The idea is that the energy that a Wiccan puts out into the world be returned in threes, so it is basically the Wiccan version of karma. If you do bad, that bad will be returned to you three times over. If you do good, that good will also be returned to you three times over.

Runes

Runes are symbols that witches commonly carve into objects. They are widely found on candles and wood.

Sabbats

The sabbats are the eight festivals that are celebrated by Wiccans. These festivals mark the seasonal changes that occur each year, and the equinoxes and the solstices mark them. On these sabbats, witches have increased power, and they have certain rituals that they will complete based on their coven. These rituals may include things like a balefire or a yule log.

Scourge

A scourge is a whip that is used by Wiccans in rituals. While this sounds harsh, often, the scourges are made of soft materials like silk because the scourge is more symbolic than anything else.

Scrying

Another method of divination is scrying. Scrying is using objects like water or a crystal ball to create visions of the future.

Séance

When you have a séance, you speak with the spirits. These spirits can either be dead people or other entities.

Shadow Work

In the Wiccan world, shadows represent the dark side of people. This does not mean that shadow work is dark magic. Rather, shadow work entails using the dark part of yourself to do good work. Shadow work can create a balance for people who have been traumatized or hurt. Shadow work is healing for witches with hurt bodies and souls because it allows them to construct something out of the darkness.

Sigils

Sigils are similar to runes because they are symbols that are used in Wiccan magic. They are drawings or other illustrations that Wiccans carry along with them to illustrate their intentions before casting a spell or brewing a potion.

Skyclad

Skyclad refers to when witches do rituals in the nude. Not all types of Wiccans do naked work, but Alexandrian Wiccans or Gardernarian Wiccans are known for working alone and doing so naked. Being naked while casting spells is not something that everyone would enjoy, but for those who do it, it is liberating, and it allows them to do magic with fewer limits.

Smudging

Smudging is the practice of using smoke or incense to cleanse places or items. It is often done with herbs as well.

Solstice

Each year, there are two solstices, and these solstices mark the shortest and longest days of the year. Solstices are vital because they align with the festivals that Wiccans celebrate.

Solar Eclipse

A solar eclipse is a special occasion for Wiccans, and it celebrates aspects of the God, such as Death and Dark Lord.

Solitary Practitioner

A solitary practitioner is a witch who works alone and is not part of a coven. Wicca is often done in covens because of how communal it is, but some people practice the teaching of Wicca without being in a formal coven. This practice may be the only option for people who are in rural places where covens aren't familiar. Some people prefer to work alone even when they have opportunities to be in covens, and that is perfectly okay.

Spell

A spell is a type of magic that uses a specific goal to drive the magic. You can accomplish a spell in millions of ways, and they often include elements such as candles, incantations, and sigils. Spells may also be done at an altar, especially when they are part of religious rituals. You can easily customize spells and make them your own.

Spirits of the Stones

The spirits of the stones means that there are energies tied to the elements of Earth, fire, air, and water that are linked to each of the four directions within the Wiccan circle.

Spiritualism

Spiritualism is believing that the dead can communicate with people who are still alive by going through mediums.

Summerlands

The Summerlands is an afterworld that is like heaven. It is often associated with reincarnation and as a break and time for rest between physical lives.

Summoner

The summoner is a male clergy member who assists the High Priest in the coven. He transmits information to the Maiden.

Talisman

A talisman is an object, usually one that is small, that witches can bring with them to places for good luck and keep bad energy away. A talisman can be pretty much anything. Even something as small as a charm or a slip of paper can be a good talisman.

Tarot Cards

Tarot cards are a method of divination. In this practice, you use a deck of 78 cards, and you turn them over to figure out what the future will hold. Tarot is a fun, easy, and inexpensive form of divination that you can start practicing right away!

The Craft

The craft is another name for witchcraft.

Transmutation

Transmutation means that one thing turns into another form. Natural objects often experience transmutation, and this property can be used in spells to do things such as turning negative energy into positive energy.

Triple Goddess

A triple goddess is one goddess that is made up of three entities. Usually, she is made up of the crone, the maiden, and the mother, who are each representative of a life stage that women go through— youth, motherhood, and old age. All these beings come together to make one single goddess.

Undine

An undine is a creature that lives in the water. Witches include nymphs and mermaids in this category.

Vision Quest

Vision questing is the process of either using astral projection or dreams to complete a specific goal. This action is also commonly known as pathworking, and it can be a highly rewarding activity for witches.

Wand

A wand is a small, thin stick usually made of wood that can hold power so that witches can focus their energy on a particular thing. The wand helps them ensure that they keep their focus on where they need it to be. Wands are not necessary, but they are fun.

Warding

Warding is a protection tactic that witches use to block off their home from negative forces. Wards are spiritual barriers that keep everyone in the home safe, which is why witches so often put them up. When you make a ward, you are keeping your vital spaces safe. Wards are particular areas that you do not want negative energies to influence.

Warlock

Warlock is a word that witches sometimes use to describe people who use magic for evil. It is not the male version of a witch. Witch is a gender-neutral term, and it applies to all Wiccans and practitioners of witchcraft. A male Wiccan would not feel comfortable if you called him a warlock because of the negative views linked to being a warlock.

Wheel of the Year

The wheel of the year is the Wiccan calendar. It is a cyclical calendar that is broken down by the eight festivals that Wiccans celebrate. The whole wheel is the entire year, completed by the eight Sabbats. The Wiccans focus on the cycle of life rather than a linear view of time. This calendar was created based on the Celtic calendar that people created before the Gregorian calendar existed.

White Magic

White magic is the opposite of black magic. When you use white magic, you choose only to use your magic for benevolent causes. You do not try to harm anyone with your powers. Wiccans use white magic and they prohibit black magic.

Wiccan Rede

The Wiccan Rede is a relevant Wiccan code that urges practitioners not to harm anyone with their magic. Wiccans are discouraged from doing any black magic, and while they are encouraged to do magic, harmful magic is inherently anti-Wicca.

Wiccaning

A wiccaning is a way of welcoming an infant into the Wiccan community. It is similar to the Christian concept of baptism. A Wiccaning is an essential rite of passage for a Wiccan family with a newborn, and during this rite, the child is given energies that will keep them safe and happy. This concept is one of the most exciting rituals in the Wiccan faith because it is a way of ushering in new life into the Wiccan covens. Children will not have to continue the Wiccan religion, but they are introduced to the community during their Wiccans. It is up to the parents whether they want to have a wiccaning at all.

Widdershins

Widdershins refers to the counter-clockwise direction. This term is used by witches in some rituals and spells, especially in the southern hemisphere. Even in the southern hemisphere, this is sometimes being replaced with clockwise motions.

Witch

To put it briefly, a witch is someone who practices witchcraft. Most Wiccans consider themselves witches (but some branches don't like the term witch), but not all witches are Wiccans. Wicca is a religion so that anyone can choose witchcraft, but not everyone will want to follow Wicca.

Witchcraft

Surely, by now, you know what witchcraft is, but it is the practice and crafting of magic.

Witches Ladder

This term is a string that has four beads in it or four knots that are sometimes used by Wiccans.

Witching Hour

This term refers to midnight.

Zodiac

The zodiac is an astrological concept that uses your birth to assign signs. The zodiac is rooted in twelve constellations and uses these constellations. Astrologers use the celestial bodies to make predictions about what people are like and what will happen to them. For many Wiccans, divine activity and astrology can be used to help with their witchcraft practices.

CHAPTER 3
Wiccan Rites and Celebrations

The Wheel of the Year

The wheel of the year refers to the Wiccan calendar that dictates when the Sabbats or the sun celebrations take place. There are also moon celebrations that occur each month during the full moon called esbats. These eight festivals are rooted in the Celtic festivals that were oriented around agriculture. Wiccans have shifted the festivals slightly and have reinvented them in ways that maintain some of the Celtic ideals but also take on a life of their own. These festivals are often times for Wiccans to practice certain rituals, but they are also times in which Wiccans are most potent.

Samhain

Samhain is a holiday that you probably already know— Halloween. It takes place on October 31st, and it marks the summer ending and the days becoming shorter. The Celts began this celebration on what is now known as All Hallows Eve, which carried into November 1st and became the Christian's All Saints' Day. Samhain is a holiday that marks people best being able to communicate with the spirits because Wiccans believe that the veil between our world and the spirit world is thinner on Samhain. For Wiccans, Samhain is the beginning of the calendar, and it represents celebrating the last of summer's bounty to enter a more scary winter.

Yule

The festival of Yule marks the winter solstice, which is the day when the night is longest. This festival occurs near December 21st, but it is slightly different each year. Another Christian holiday closely aligns with this one— Christmas— showing how pre-Christian religions influence many of the Christian festivals. Yule is one of the quieter festivals, and there are less gatherings around this time. Wiccans will give fights around this time and light candles on Midwinter Eve. They even use pine decorations and holly! If you've ever heard of a yule log, it is through pagan tradition that the idea came to be. In old times, pagans would burn a log to represent the holiday.

Imbolc

Imbolc is the third Wiccan holiday that takes place on February 1. It marks the beginning of spring, even though February doesn't feel like spring in most of the world. Again, it corresponds with the Christian feast day of St. Brigid, who legend says was based on the Celtic goddess Brigid. Imbolc is all about things reawakening and life starting to flourish again after the long winter. Many new members of individual covens are brought in around this time, and a lot of the rituals include lighting candles. It is a time to get back to focusing on the Wiccan religion and reorient your perspective.

Ostara

Ostara is a holiday that takes place around March 21, and it aligns with the spring equinox. The Christians have Easter, but Wiccans have Ostara. Ostara is a festival that marks fertility because, during this time, you can start to see spring come into bloom. In ancient times, this fertility was often represented by bunnies and eggs, which you see carry on into modern times. During this holiday, the Goddess is said to be in her maiden form. She and the young God are getting closer to conceiving their child who is said to be born on Yule. Ostara is a time for Wiccans to realign themselves with what they want to accomplish and send life through those goals. It is about reviving and reenergizing things that winter had left stagnant and slow.

Beltane

Beltane is the last of the three fertility festivals that usher in spring, and it occurs on May 1st. The veil between the spirit and mortal world is again thinner on Beltane because Beltane is the polar opposite of Samhain on the calendar. For Wiccans, this festival is often highly sexual because it was when the Maiden Goddess and the God went through the great rite (marriage), and their union marked the culmination of the growing fertility from the months prior. Beltane often is a fun festival that includes things like bonfires and sleeping under the stars. It is a typical time for handfasting and finding love.

Litha

Litha, also Midsummer, marks the summer solstice, which is usually around June 21st. The God is most powerful on this day because it marks the day when the days stop growing longer and begin to dwindle. Litha is a festival that celebrates the brightness of summer and often includes bonfires to hold onto the summer light for as long as possible. Further, it marks the coming harvest. Wiccans commonly do rituals outside during Litha, and they are filled with joy. Also, they make the most of the spells that use the sun. It is no doubt the brightest of Wiccan holidays.

Lammas

Lammas occurs on August 1, and it represents the beginning of harvest. Grain would be collected during this time, and people would be able to bake bread after not having fresh grain all winter. In some traditions, it is called Lughnasadh from the Celtic god, Lugh. During this time the Sun God becomes weaker, and he starts to make his descent towards death before being revived when Yule comes around. Lammas is a time when Wiccans are thankful. It is a great time for an appreciation ceremony. It was an important time for ancient people, and it continues to be important to pagans today.

Mabon

Mabon is the final festival on the Wiccan calendar, and it occurs around September 21, during the autumnal equinox. This festival marks the time when winter is coming near, but it is still a time of harvest when nuts and fruits are ready to be collected. During this time, Wiccans often look back at the year and celebrate what their work has brought them. It is a time of great abundance, which means that it is a good time for spells that are related to prosperity. It is also a good time for being gracious. Mabon is often bittersweet because it marks the decline towards winter. Many Wiccans bake a lot during this time and have foods made from the goods of harvest. They also use cornucopias as centerpieces. They indulge in cider and pies, and they preserve fruits and vegetables throughout the year. This festival also marks the cycle of old age for the deities. Wiccans may spend this time appreciating the outdoors while they still can or giving offerings to their altar. It is one of the last holidays that they can do extensive outdoor activities. Cities also have ceremonies and festivities to celebrate Pagan Pride Day during Mabon.

Wiccan Rites

Like any religion, Wicca has rites of passage that Wiccans celebrate. During these times, they go through certain rituals that the elders of the community will guide, and everyone will take part in it. These rituals are outside of the holidays, but they take place near the festivals and are used as part of the festival celebrations as well. These rites are important to Wiccans, and they allow Covens to change and grow. Further, they enable witchcraft to spread and to flourish. Without rites, Wicca would be lacking many of the religious qualities that makes it appeal to so many people who are looking for direction

Dedication

The dedication ceremony is a ceremony that marks a Wiccan deciding to become dedicated to the Wiccan religion and the deities. This ceremony can happen when there is a new moon, but it can also occur whenever the person chooses and feels that they want to be dedicated to the Wiccan faith. This ceremony will require incense, sacred oil, and candles. It is done around the altar. The dedication marks a member's beginning with the Wiccan faith, and it allows them to become part of a community that is bigger than themselves.

Wiccaning

Wiccanings are a way of welcoming a newborn into the Wiccan community. Sometimes, it is called a "baby-naming ceremony" or a sainting. This practice is similar to the Christian celebration of baptism. Although, when a child goes through a Wiccaning, they do not have to belong to the Wiccan faith. Wicca emphasizes that each person in Wicca must determine themselves that they want to be part of it. Thus, the child may choose to join Wicca, but they are not committed to it. A high priest or priestess commits this rite, but it can also be done by the parents of the child sometimes. This ceremony also gives other members of the coven a chance to bless the child and celebrate that child.

Handfasting

Handfasting is the Wiccan equivalent to a marriage ceremony. It represents two people being linked together. People who choose to partake in this do not need to have the intention of getting legally married, but they also may use it as an opportunity to wed as well legally. This ceremony is generally completed by members of the clergy, often a high priest or priestess. It is rooted in Celtic traditions that called for people's arms to be tied together with ribbon to represent being unified forever, which is why today we call marriage "tying the knot." This rite can be custom fit to what you want it to be to match your expectations for your handfasting.

Handparting

Handparting is the opposite of handfasting. It is a ceremony that Wiccans use to divorce people when they were unified in a handfasting ceremony. It also does not count as a legal divorce. Usually, a Wiccan leader will complete this ceremony. It is done using the ribbon that was used for the couple's handfasting ceremony. The relationship is then severed. It is a somewhat sad ceremony, but it allows couples to part and move on with their lives without having an unwanted connection, so while it is bittersweet, it is sometimes needed.

Appreciation

An appreciation rite is a rite that Wiccans use when they want to show respect to the natural world as well as the divine and spirit worlds. This ritual is all about gratitude, and it is a way that Wiccans reassert everything that they believe in. Wiccans can choose what they want to be grateful for based on their type of Wicca and what their coven decides. There are no firm rules. This rite is often practiced on sabbats, especially during harvest, but it is appropriate at any time.

Funeral

In the Wiccan religion, a funeral is commonly called a Summerland service. This rite marks the end of a person's life. A Wiccan funeral is similar to most other funerals in that it allows people to celebrate the life of the dead and to remember stories about that person. This ceremony allows healing to begin and can include several qualities such as poetry, eulogies, and prayers.

CHAPTER 4
Mesmerizing Magic

Types of Witches

Within the Wiccan witch distinction, there are several other types of witches that you can be based on the types of witchcraft that you can do. You don't have to identify as one of these types, but these types can help you understand what you like to do most in witchcraft and find other people who have similar interests. These types of witches mainly help you see the variety of spells and attitudes that witches can have. They can all use crystals as part of their craft, but they have different areas of emphasis when they use those crystals.

Cottage Witches

A cottage witch is a witch who is energized by pursuits related to the home. They often do most of their spells in the home, and they enjoy making their homesteads and the people in them happy. People who enjoy domestic activities are likely to be cottage witches, also known as hearth witches. These witches will want to make sure their homes are extra protected, and they will tend to use tools like brooms or other homestead items in their spells. While cottage witches are not limited by religion, they can be Wiccan if they choose.

Crystal Witches

There is a special distinction of witches who tend to use crystals primarily in their work. Any other witch category can include the use of crystals, but crystal witches use crystals in most or all of their spells. If you are interested in crystals, you don't have to identify as a crystal witch, but if you find yourself drawn to crystals and want to work with them constantly, this may be a perfect distinction for you. Crystal witches will use several methods that include crystals such as crystal therapy or crystal in meditation. A crystal witch would feel incomplete without their crystals.

Eclectic Witches

Eclectic witches are witches who combine different parts of witchcraft and have no main area of focus. They like to try a myriad of methods, and they go by whatever feels right for them at the time. Most witches probably fall into this category. Wiccans who don't fall into other categories often just call themselves Wiccan rather than eclectic.

Green Witches

Green witches are witches that have a special connection with nature. They love to keep plants around and often have fresh herbs that they use in their spells. Green witches often will use a combination of herbs and crystals when they are doing crystal magic, but they may also channel other natural elements. Green witches love the great outdoors, so they may practice their witchcraft outside and away from their houses to feel more connected to greenery.

Hedge Witches

Hedge witches are witches who combine the elements of cottage witches and green witches. They like natural features, including crystals, but they also want to focus on their homesteads and their relationships to spirits. These witches were seen initially as wise old women, and they got their name from living just beyond villages (they were on the hedge between the village and the natural world). They combine the appeals of nature and the home, and they like to incorporate magic in every part of their lives. Often, they do want to work alone, but some hedge witches do join covens and are part of religions like Wicca.

Kitchen Witches

Kitchen witches are similar to cottage witches, but they focus on the domestic duties of the kitchen. They often love to use spells that relate to cooking and use cauldrons frequently. They spend much of their time in their kitchens, and they can use crystals to improve the quality of their meals and other concoctions. Some kitchen witches will keep their altar in their kitchen, and they will probably cast most of their spells there, even the non-kitchen related ones. These witches make great dinner party hosts! Like green witches, they may like to mix herbs or other edible elements with their crystals to prepare for more powerful spells.

Spirit Working Witches

Spirit working witches are witches who often participate in necromancy and other elements of the spirit world. They strive to communicate with spirits and use psychic abilities to connect with the dead. They often use crystal magic in their practice both for spells, maintaining good energies, and scrying.

Tasks to Get Started

Readying Your Altar

You will need to start preparing your altar by determining what space you want to have your altar in. It can be any space that you choose. You can use a full room to hold your altar, or you can use just a tiny portion of that room. It doesn't matter what you choose to be the space as your altar. As long as your area fits your needs, it is perfect. You don't need to make a massive investment of your space or get a new house to have a sufficient altar. Work with what you have and go from there.

What you need for the altar itself is a space that is a flat space. You can use things such as a table, a box, or a desk, among other things. Try to ensure that your space isn't made of a material that would conduct electricity for safety reasons because your tools may be conducive. Again, you don't have to have the world's prettiest altar. If you have the resources to make it look nicer, that is great, but the point of the altar is for worship. It doesn't have to win any prizes. Make your altar something that fits your tastes because you have to live with it.

You'll want to try to set up your altar in a room that you have cleansed with sea salt or another cleansing agent of your choice. You'll also want to cast a purification spell on the room. If you can set up your altar outdoors, you will not have to cleanse or purify your space because it is part of nature. You'll want to set up the altar in the middle of the room and ensure that when you look at the altar, you are looking towards the east.

In the space around the altar, you should draw a circle, which is an important circle in the Wiccan rituals. You can make this circle using various things like chalk, but it can also be drawn only in your imagination. Do whatever makes you feel most comfortable in your worship or follow whatever your type of Wiccanism suggests.

You'll need various tools and adornments for your altar based on the type of Wicca you practice. The Gardnerians, for example, need eight tools while the Saxons only need a knife, a spear, and a sword. You could even choose to branch out from all other denominations and make up your own rules and choose whatever equipment you want to use when you practice Wicca. You will want to make sure that your tools are cleansed before you use and you'll also want to charge them with energy.

Most witches across Wiccan denominations will require a special knife, called an athame, in their craft. It is sometimes referred to by different names in various types of Wicca, but the knife should be something that you like and fits you individually. You can choose how big the knife is and what style of handle you want. You can buy the knife online or in stores. It doesn't have to be a special knife beyond the special attributes that you give it through your magic. If you can, you'll want to have your Wiccan name etched into the blade of the knife. Or, if you can't have it engraved, you can put your name on any part of it by writing your name in marker or using a label. Some other tools that you may need for use at your altar are a wand, a bell, a sword, and a pentacle. Again, this will vary depending on your practice. You may also be required to wear a robe or practice skyclad.

You'll want to have certain adornments for your altar to ensure that it is ready for use. Many witches like to have candles and incense on their altars because Wiccans often use both incense and candles in their practices. White candles are always good options because they are the most versatile, but different candles will have different meanings, as will various incenses.

You will also want a few dishes to hold things like salt and water as well as a libation dish, which is a dish that is used when Wiccans first pour their ritual wine/fruit juice for a ritual to the gods.

Relatedly, you'll also want goblets for the same ritual. The high priest or priestess will have their goblets on the altar.

Additionally, you can place representations of the deities onto your altar. They can be whatever objects you want that remind you of the deities. They can be using photos, statues, or representative objects. Feel free to be creative with these items.

Wiccans traditionally follow specific rules for their altars, so follow those as best as you are able based on your type of Wiccanism. You should also know that as long as you are worshipping candidly, your efforts are valid even if they don't follow the letter of the law. Wiccanism, especially as a broad concept, is open to possibility and is flexible. However, some traditional practices of it will be more rigid.

Keep an Open Mind

When you begin witchcraft, you will need to keep an open mind. Many people close themselves off to the possibility of witchcraft before they have even considered it properly. Your magic will be limited. It isn't like what you see in movies about witches. It is much more subtle, but it is still well worth the effort that you will put into it. Don't close your mind off because you feel silly or assume witchcraft isn't for you. Witchcraft and Wicca are for everyone who wants to take part.

CHAPTER 5
Crystal Magic

Crystals are some of the most magnificent tools that you can use in Wiccan witchcraft. They contain so much power and possibility. It can take some time to get used to using crystals and to figure out how to best use them to your advantage, but it is well worth the effort that you will put in. Crystals will help keep you safe, allow you to manifest your dreams, and help you combat normal life problems that may stand in your way of happiness. These crystals, radiant stones, come in a variety of forms, and each form can be used for various purposes. Much of crystal magic is personalized based on a witch's experiences, but there are some common associations and basic rules that most Wiccans follow when it comes to crystal magic.

History of Crystal Magic

People have been using crystals to create magic for thousands of years, and they have done so without having to stop and think about it. It came naturally. Before crystals themselves were recognized, stone was acknowledged, which is a broader group that crystals fall under. These stones were seen as a way to build early societies, and some of the first buildings were religious in nature, showing how stones were immediately used as a way of worship. The stones connected the natural world to realms far beyond the Earth's plane. People were already learning that through the parts of the Earth, they could connect to things far beyond themselves. Stones were transformative in ways that excited humans.

The magic of stone was first recognized (or at least the first that we know of) 11,000 years ago when a temple was built from stone in Turkey. Further, humans continued to recognize the amazing properties of the stones that were part of our Earth as they continued to build sacred places from stone and eventually began to build houses from the stone. Stone remains an integral part of our lives. It builds the world around us, and it is a tool we have taken from earth to protect ourselves. It represents our alignment with our Earth and our ability to harness parts of the Earth to use the Earth's energies to our advantage.

Stones started to grow far beyond parts for shelter. They became sacred. People began carrying stones with them for luck, and they began to see that there was more to stone than they realized. Soon, they would start seeing the beautiful wonder of crystals, which help so much more power than early humans would have ever guessed. The early wishing stones that humans carried were not quite as beautiful as the crystals we know today, but they were still precious, and they would bring good fortune upon the people who carried them.

Remember that Wiccans believe that non-living things still have energies, which includes stones. Among the stones are some of the most precious stones that exist, which are crystals. Crystals are stones that are generally found in huge mounds of rock, and they were made from minerals below the Earth's surface. After years of formulating, crystals formed and became stones filled with color, looking more magical than ever. Early people recognized with wonderment what the pretty stones could do right away. Aboriginal people embraced crystals, as did people in ancient Greece, Rome, and Egypt. They would carry the crystals around as talismans, and the gems became an essential part of their rituals, including death rituals.

Crystals continue to be relevant to people who have found new ways to tap into the power of crystals. We have discovered the healing properties of crystals and the ability to balance ourselves with them. Through magic, we can realign our energies and reduce all the negativity in our lives. Crystals don't just help one part of our lives, but they tap into each component and allow us to engage with ourselves and others in unique ways. Wiccans use crystals in special ways. Some people limit their crystal use to only healing, but Wiccans use them in most parts of their practice. They use them for rituals and spells. They incorporate them into as many areas of their lives as possible and they use those crystals to get in touch with the divine. There's no limit to what a Wiccan can do with crystals. Crystals are a magnificent part of Earth, so they can be used to better our connection to all parts of existence, and we can learn through crystals how to help ourselves and others thrive merely by embracing the energies around us.

Commonly Used Crystals

If you want to use crystals properly, it helps to know which crystals are some of the most prominent and powerful ones that Wiccans and other witches commonly use. Further, it helps to understand the general symbolism and powers that the gems contain because by knowing this, you will be able to craft your spells beyond the ones provided in this book. While it does help to be given some starting spells, part of the joy of witchcraft is learning to craft your own magic given the tools around you. While there are organized aspects of Wicca, there are still many personal liberties that allow you to be creative with your witchcraft. You can use crystals in conjunction with other magical elements such as candles, spells, or sigils, but crystals are also pretty compelling on their own, so it's up to you to decide how they best work for you! There's no right or wrong way to practice magic (beyond the Wiccan Rede), so it will take some experimentation before you know what you like best.

Amber

Amber is actually not a crystal, but although it is the sap from a tree, it can be used as a crystal in witchcraft because of its crystal-like properties. This crystal's chakra is the solar plexus, so it is especially helpful in spells that help you with willpower or tasks associated with your personality because the solar plexus is the central part of your personality. Amber can also be beneficial in improving your self-confidence. Amber is an easy crystal to find, and it can both amplify and absorb energy. It works well on its own, but it also pairs well with clear quartz (aka quartz crystal). Its honey-colored appearance makes it quite recognizable.

Amethyst

Amethyst is one of the most popular and pretty of all the magical crystals (and other stones that are grouped in with crystals). This stone is the gemstone of Aquarians, who might find it extra powerful. It is a purple color, and this color can range from being a light to a deep purple. It is ruled by the third-eye of the chakra and the crown chakra, meaning that it is associated with both insight into the internal and external worlds, but it also helps us stay aligned with nature and grounded to the Earth. It also provides internal peace.

Amethyst is a stone that's known for accomplishing many things beyond what. It is known to help people with addictions or who struggle to balance healthy and indulgent parts of themselves because it was often known to ancient Greeks as a "sober stone," because it was said to help ameliorate the negative effects of alcohol. Further, this stone's high vibration means that it is great at converting negative energy into positive energy. It also helps magnify intelligence, intuition, and psychic skills. Thus, amethyst is one of the most transformative stones there is. It helps spiritually guide people and heals them. It is one of the most versatile crystals, which means you'll probably want to have it around.

To sum up the key pluses of amethyst, some of the main ways that this crystal can help you with are sleep issues, being more creative, balancing your worry, and helping you with addiction. This crystal also works well with clear quartz and citrine. The more you practice using amethyst, the better you will become at tapping into all of its power. Not only does it look pretty, but it can transform your life.

Ametrine

Ametrine is a special crystal that is the combination of citrine and amethyst. Thus, this crystal will have both the yellow and the purple parts of it that represent each gem that it contains. Further, ametrine allows you to combine the properties of citrine and amethyst and magnify their impacts for amazing results. As a combination crystal, you can get more bang for your buck, and moreover, this gem is gorgeous, so it would be nice to look at even if its magical qualities weren't so great.

Ametrine is associated with all the chakra that citrine and amethyst are, so it rules over the solar plexus, the third-eye, and the crown. Thus, it is linked to having plenty, lessening negativity, creating balance among energies, handling personality, and enabling psychic powers. Citrine can be used in conjunction with citrine, amethyst, and clear quartz to tap into its power even more!

Apatite

Apatite is a gem that is a bluish-green hue. Unlike most gems, it is best to store this one by itself because it is soft and easily damaged. This stone is usually used for spells that lead to people having greater wisdom or searching for the truth. It is associated with several parts of the chakra— heart, solar plexus, throat, or crown. Accordingly, it combines different parts of your being to provide further clarity and wisdom. It can be useful when you are meditating or it can help reduce your anxiety if you carry it with you. It can also help you in pursuits that require you to uncover unfound truths by magnifying your intuition and cosmically leading you to answers. Apatite can be used with clear quartz, amethyst, or rose quartz.

Aquamarine

Aquamarine is another blue crystal with greenish tones. It is known for helping people who are feeling worried or who have fears, but it can also be a powerful protection crystal. It is a crystal that tends to amplify, and it is associated with the heart, third-eye, and throat chakras. Therefore, it helps people calm down, feel braver, and have a better understanding of their spiritual selves. It works well with turquoise, clear quartz, and amethyst.

Black Tourmaline

Black Tourmaline is a gem that absorbs energies. Thus, it is great to take around with you if you need protection from negative forces because it will absorb those negative energies rather than sending out good ones to reduce the impact of the bad ones. If you break this gem, you should bury it in the Earth and get a new one so that the negative energy doesn't influence you. This black crystal can be used with clear quartz, and it is associated with the root chakra. Consequently, it is one of the crystals that is most linked with your Earthly connection and your physical body.

Tourmaline can also come in other colors (such as a pink and green color) that are beautiful and can be used in similar fashions to tourmaline, but those will have other chakras based on their color. I love watermelon tourmaline, which is great if you want to manifest a romantic relationship (or for platonic love as well).

Bloodstone

This crystal is sometimes known as heliotrope, and it is a brownish-green color, although it does have various shades that may differ slightly and include specs of red or gold. It was named for a Christian story about the crucifixion of Jesus Christ. It is said that Jesus's blood dropped on green stones, which was said to explain the red specks sometimes found in bloodstone. For Wiccans, it is used to help practitioners move past their negative emotions so that they can unveil the truth and gain the wisdom that they need to help them through their difficult situations. Thus, this stone is perfect when you need to make a decision, and when you feel lost in your emotions.

Carnelian

Carnelian is part of the quartz family, and it is a type of chalcedony. This stone is commonly linked to bravery, and it can help you resist your weaknesses and improve upon them. This crystal is absorbent of energy, and it is associated with the root and sacral chakras. Thus, it is ideal when you need to accomplish tasks that make you feel petrified, when you need to add more passion to your relationships, or when you need to discover who you are. This gem can be used with sardonyx, malachite, or clear quartz.

Chalcedony

This stone is part of the quartz family, and is generally a light blue color. It is called the "speaker's stone," because it allows you to say what you need to say and enunciate your points better. Chalcedony amplifies energy, and it is associated with the throat chakra.

Citrine

Citrine is another one of the most important gems that you will encounter. It is usually yellow, but it is an incredibly translucent yellow. It can either be created or is sometimes naturally occurring. This gem amplifies energy, and it is associated with the solar plexus chakra. Witches commonly place this around their home to create a better home atmosphere. It is known for bringing prosperity, boosting self-confidence, helping with manifestation, and creating a generous spirit. You can place citrine in the corners of your rooms to ensure that you have good energies in your homestead.

Danburite

This crystal comes in many colors that are associated with various chakras. All danburite varieties are linked to being spiritually aware and finding a connection with your higher power. It comes in shades of gray, green, or clear. Green is associated with the heart while the others are associated with the crown. This gem can facilitate unconditional love, make changes easier, reduce stress, cleanse the spaces it is in, and being a high vibration crystal, it can help you connect with the God and the Goddess. Further, you can use this stone with other stones that have high vibrations such as moldavite or phenacite.

Emerald

Emerald is well-known by jewelers, but it is also a vital gem for witches. Witches can buy polished gemstones or they can buy rawer versions of the gem for their practice. This gem is known for its breathtaking green color, and it is a form of beryl, which is a mineral that also makes gems like aquamarine or morganite. Emerald is linked to the heart chakra, which is why it is commonly worn as jewelry, and it is associated with romantic success, unconditional love, and divine love. It is also known as a great gem for protection, recovering from trauma, having spiritual awareness, being kind, and forgiving others. It works well with pink stones, green stones, clear quartz, or other beryls. Emerald is one of my favorite gems because it represents many elements, such as love, kindness, and romance, that I value most.

Epidote

Epidote, like emerald, is a green gem that is linked to the heart chakra. It represents many of the same qualities as the emerald, and it is known for being used between partners to balance their love and effectuate growth between them. This is an amplifying gem, and it is great for healing broken relationships. It can be used with any amplifying stones. Additionally, for people who live in urban areas, this stone is a great choice if you feel like you need more connection to nature.

Fuchsite

This is yet another green gem that is linked to the heart chakra. It is also an absorbing gem. Most commonly, it is used with the ruby to amplify the ruby's power. Frequently, it is worn in a piece of jewelry. This stone is known for its ability to protect and heal. It is a rejuvenating stone and allows growth to come from what has wilted. It is a soft crystal, so you may want to store it separately from your other crystals.

Fluorite

Fluorite is another one of the most common gems that witches use. It is fascinating because of the wide range of colors that it comes in. You can see it in green or purple, and the best type of fluorite for magic is probably the rainbow fluorite that has a variety of colors in it. It is associated with several chakras— throat, crown, third-eye, and heart. It is a great gem to use if you feel the distance between your body and your spirit. Further, it is great for interacting with divine entities, and it can help you bring harmony into your life.

Garnet

Garnet comes in a variety of colors, usually autumn colors like red, yellow, and orange. Garnets amplify energy, and they are associated with different chakras based on their color. Red is associated with the root chakra, green garnets are associated with the heart chakra, and the others are associated with the sacral chakra. Garnets are used for witches to expand their ideas and to prevent themselves from becoming limited. They are also good for benefitting your career. You can use garnets with other colored garnets, and you can use them with both clear and smoky quartz. They are transitional gems, so they are also great when you are going through a period of change.

Howlite

Howlite is a gemstone that is often colored turquoise, but in its natural form, it is mostly colorless or has very little color. This crystal is known for its association with divine entities. It can be used to feel more aligned with the divine. Being a crystal that absorbs, it will take in bad energies, especially overwhelming feelings like anger. It is associated with the crown chakra, and it can be used in correspondence with amethyst and turquoise.

Hematite

Hematite is one of the essential gemstones that I suggest you have in your collection. It absorbs energy, and it is a black stone that will have other colors that run through it, which you can see when you put it in the light. This stone is great when you need to detoxify from negative energies, and it is also great for when you are feeling stressed or like you are ungrounded. It pairs well with either malachite or lapis lazuli.

Jade

Jade is a lovely gemstone that has been long used for its helpful properties. It was even used in ancient times. Jade is known for being green, but it can also come in other hues like orange or white. You have to be careful with jade stones because this crystal is often reproduced, so you must be sure to find genuine jade. Jade absorbs energy, and it is associated with several chakras based on the colors that you have it in. The most common color, green, is related to the heart, but other colors are associated with the root (gray, black, or red), sacral (orange), solar plexus (yellow), crown (white), or third eye (purple). Jade is ideal if you have negative, recurring thoughts that you need to break, and it is good when you need to calm your guilty conscience. Further, it can help your life force and decrease your greed. Finally, it is great for spells regarding love, of any kind. It pairs well with other colors of jade, malachite, and clear quartz.

Jasper

While you might not have heard of this crystal before, it is highly beneficial to have in your collection. Jasper is formed by the combination of different stones like quartz or chalcedony. It comes in a wide range of colors and forms, and it a stone that absorbs energy. Its chakras are linked based on the color that it is. Jasper is the following chakras: third-eye or throat (blue), heart (green), solar plexus (brown or yellow), sacral (orange), or root (red). This stone is excellent for people with mental health issues because it is good for when you have too much energy that results in negative behaviors like eating disorders, addiction, obsessive-compulsive disorder, or anxiety. It can be used with other colors of Jasper, or it can be used with black tourmaline.

Jet

Jet is another lesser-known "crystal" that can have heaps of influence on you and your life. Technically, a jet is not a stone, but it is an honorary one in the world of witchcraft. It is actually pieces of driftwood that have become fossils. Nevertheless, it has long been used to better the well being of people. It is a transmuting stone because it started as wood and then became another substance. This gem can help you stay clearheaded, and it allows you to find mental clarity even in the most chaotic of situations. It is one of the best stones that you can use if you are feeling overwhelmed by grief or sadness. It is also good for protecting your house from harmful spirits and other negative energies.

Kyanite

This brittle crystal is usually found in blue, but it also comes in other shades. Kyanite is frequently shaped to look like a blade, and it is special in that it holds no energy, so you will never need to cleanse it. It is mostly related to the throat chakra, and it can be used to break the stagnancy of your life and to forge new opportunities for you or your loved ones. If you feel stuck in place, kyanite is a great option to get you back on track. It is also great for promoting healthy communication and dependability. You can use it with other colors of kyanite or with you can use it to transfer energy from one crystal to another.

Labradorite

Labradorite is a stone that looks like a normal rock often, but it can shine when it is polished and cut. It looks like moonstones, and First Nation people believed that it connected the earth plane to the other planes of existence. It is associated with the third eye or the throat chakras. Thus, it can be good for enhancing magical attributes, lessening the bad parts of your personality, helping you cleanse yourself of things that you are addicted to, and can help you act less impulsive. Most importantly, perhaps, you can use this to connect with realms other than the Earth realm. You can use this stone in conjunction with amethyst, sodalite, or clear quartz.

Lapis Lazuli

Lapis Lazuli is another object that isn't technically a crystal, but it does have attributes that make it similar to a crystal, and it has been used as a crystal for centuries. This rock absorbs energy, and it is often blue. It is connected to the throat, and it is associated with communication of all kinds. It was even found in the tomb of King Tutankhamen! This can be used with other gems like malachite.

Malachite

Malachite is a vital crystal that many witches like to keep handy. This is a green crystal that absorbs energy. Like many other green crystals, it is associated with the heart chakra. It is known for its association with travel, and it can be used to help you feel more self-assured when you are going to unknown places. It is also useful for blocking pollutants and protecting you from unforeseen incidents. Many witches like to carry this with them when they get on a plane or other modes of transportation. You can use this with lapis lazuli.

Moonstone

Moonstone is a milky stone that is usually white or black. It can help you form bonds with the divine and your intuition. Further, it protects you through amplifying goof energy. It is also great for when you need a creative solution to a problem that you have. Moonstone is associated with the third eye or the crown. It can be used harmoniously with either amethyst or rose quartz.

Onyx

Another black gem is onyx, and it is a type of chalcedony. This stone absorbs energy, and Wiccans commonly associate it with the root chakra. It is linked with sexuality, so it can be used to better your sexual or romantic relationships. It is good to ensure that any excess sexual feelings are balanced, and it reduces the friction in relationships. Further, it is useful if you need more self-control. You can use this gem with carnelian. It is common for Wiccans to put this gem near their beds to maintain their sexual relationships and to keep nightmares at bay.

Peridot

Peridot is a green gemstone that represents many critical emotional areas such as mercy, love, and passion. Peridot is associated with the heart chakra and amplifies romantic energies.

If you would like to be more forgiving, peridot is perfect for you. Further, it can make you feel more compassion for others while reducing your ego. It is an excellent gemstone if you want to ease your traumas and balance your chakras. With peridot, you can cleanse your aura and create more harmony in your life. It is also a great luck booster! You can use peridot in conjunction with any type of quartz.

Quartz Crystal

Quartz crystal, or clear quartz, is perhaps the most important crystal of all for many witches. It is often the crystal that beginner Wiccans start with because it has the most possibilities, and it can be used in a myriad of ways. One of the perks of this crystal is that it will cleanse itself, and it can be used to cleanse other crystals as well (more on cleansing later). This crystal is an amplifier, and it can be used with pretty much any crystal to make the other crystal more powerful. This reasoning is why it's probably the most vital crystal in a witch's collection if you were to rate the importance of the crystals (which I generally don't like to do). It is mostly associated with the crown, but it has connections to all the other chakras as well, which feeds its versatility.

Clear quartz is an excellent gem for connecting to the divine as well as other planes of existence. Further, it can be used to cleanse other objects you are using for your spells. It also is known for providing mental clarity to witches by harmonizing the connection between your body and your mind. Accordingly, it is great to use when you meditate or to keep around you so that you constantly have an object of clarity nearby. The use of clear quartz is nearly endless, and you can use it instead of several more specific crystals when you are in a pinch. If you need an all-purpose crystal, this is perfect. Because it pairs well with all other crystals, it will never interfere with your spells to have clear quartz around.

Rhodochrosite

Rhodochrosite is one of the crystals that I find to be the most beautiful. It is a vibrant pink stone that you could think was rose quartz in its lighter forms, but rhodochrosite usually is more intense in its color, and it has white stripes on it. This crystal amplifies energy, and you can link it to the root and the heart chakras. It is associated with love and kindness. You can also use it to purify your aura. Further, not only does it help you love others, but it helps you to have more compassion for yourself as well, so if you are struggling to love yourself, this gem is ideal for you. You can use it with either clear or rose quartz to add to its power.

Rose Quartz

Rose quartz is another type of quartz that Wiccan witches commonly use. It represents similar ideas as rhodochrosite, such as kindness and love. It is associated with the heart chakra, as many pink stones are, and it is suitable for healing pains related to lost love, such as death or a breakup. By amplifying energy, this stone can help link you with other people and deepen the compassion that you have for them. It can also give you more inner peace and help you be more lighthearted, even in the face of grief. You can use rose quartz with many other crystals like peridot, amethyst, and clear quartz.

Ruby

Ruby is a crystal that comes in vibrant red colors. Like sapphires, a ruby is a version of corundum. Rubies are associated with the chakras of root and heart, and they are linked to all things regarding the heart. They can facilitate divine love. They can also help you get through the more challenging parts of love. For example, they can help you be more emotionally intimate, and they can help you better show your love to your loved ones. Rubies also allow you to embrace feelings that you have tried to repress and ignore, and they will enable you to become more content with those feelings. You can use rubies with rose quartz and sapphires.

Sapphire

Sapphire is a gemstone that many people know, but they often don't realize the amazing attributes that it has. Sapphires can come in many colors, but they are most commonly known for being blue. The blue form represents the third eye or the throat while the pink represents the third eye, the orange represents the sacral, and the yellow represents the solar plexus. The sapphire allows you both to manifest and to protect yourself. It is also great to help you better express yourself and be candid about your feelings. It also helps you relinquish control so that you can let the divine take over and fill you with courage and skill. You can use the sapphire with a ruby.

Sodalite

Sodalite is a blue gem that you can use to amplify energies that you want to be more prominent parts of yourself. This crystal allows you to balance energy so you do not have too much or too little of anything. These gems are great for people who have trouble balancing their moods. It is excellent to use this gem with amethyst.

Smoky Quartz

Smoky quartz is a type of quartz that is used less than clear quartz and rose quartz. Nevertheless, it is still valuable. Smoky quartz turns negative energy into positive energy via transmutation. Smoky quartz usually looks to be gray or brown, and it is associated with the root or crown chakra. You can use it whenever you need to instill more positive energy into your life. It works well with amethyst, clear quartz, and citrine.

Tiger's Eye

Tiger's eye has one of the most intriguing names of all crystals. It is named because it actually looks like the eye of a tiger. It absorbs energy, and you can find it in three colors: red, yellow, and blue. The red is related to the root, the yellow is associated with the solar plexus, and the blue is associated with the throat. You can connect this crystal to all things about the self. If you have a problem with yourself, this is the gem you would want to use. It can help you find self-love and to stop having so much self-criticism.

Further, it can help you create self-compassion and build self-compassion. If you feel lost and don't know who you are, it will help you build a sense of self so that you can have self-worth and self-esteem. It works well with citrine. For health reasons, you should try to use tiger's eye that has been polished because it contains asbestos, which can be harmful if you aren't careful. When it is polished, the asbestos is gone.

Topaz

Topaz is an amplifying gem that comes in several colors, most notably gold or brown, but also is commonly blue. It can be related to the sacral part of you, but based on the color can also be related to the root, the third eye, the solar plexus, the throat, the heart, or the crown. Like tiger's eye, you can use it to help you with yourself and things like self-esteem and expression.

Turquoise

Turquoise is another great crystal. Initially, it served as an essential crystal for soldiers, and it was said to protect warriors from harm. Today, it is still a protective crystal that many use when they need power for themselves and their safety. It's also suitable for protecting relationships and dealing with all kinds of fights. Personal battles and public battles are both issues that you can improve with turquoise. It absorbs energy, and it is a bluish-green color that links it to the throat chakra. You can use it with onyx or clear quartz.

Beyond these crystals listed, there are many more that can have various properties, but these are the major ones that are used by Wiccans and other witches in crystal magic, but you should not limit yourself to just these. Explore your different avenues once you are better established as a crystal practitioner, but for now, these crystals give you the understanding you need as a beginner practitioner.

Crystal Systems

Crystals all have different properties not only by what kind of stone they are and what color they are but also because of how they are shaped. Take note of the shapes of crystals and what those shapes mean to better understand how you can use your crystals to the fullest. While you don't need to know too in-depth what these groups entail, it helps to have a general idea of the classifications of crystals, especially when you start preparing to buy crystals and compare them.

Hexagonal crystals are known for manifestation powers. Meanwhile, isometric crystals are known for bettering hardships, and they also tend to amplify energy. Orthorhombic crystals are cleansing, and triclinic crystals keep bad energies away. Amorphous crystals have dynamic properties. Tetragonal crystals attract other things. Further, trigonal crystals are food for manifestation and protection. Finally, the monoclinic group is good for your intuition.

Hexagonal crystals include beryl, dolomite, quartz, and cinnabar. Isometric crystals include garnet, fluorite, lapis lazuli, and sodalite. Orthorhombic crystals include peridot, iolite, and olivine. Triclinic crystals include turquoise and kyanite. Amorphous minerals include jet and amber. Tetragonal crystals include Zircon, idocrase, and scapolite. Trigonal crystals include rubies and sapphires. The monoclinic system includes moonstone and malachite.

If you don't have certain stones that a spell calls for, you can swap them out for other similar stones that have similar properties and purposes. Use your best judgement and you will probably still have stellar results. Many stones have overlap in their functions, so don't be too rigid with your uses of the stones and try to discover as many ways that they can be used as possible. The more you explore crystal magic, the more clearly you'll see that what crystals you have doesn't matter as much as how you use them because it is your power that taps into the magical qualities crystals possess. It is not their powers that fuel you.

Preparations
Obtaining Crystals

When you first start out, it can be overwhelming to see the long list of crystals that you could buy. Crystals can be expensive, and if you are on a budget, you may think that you'll never be able to do crystal magic. Fear not, though, that is not the case. You don't need to be rich or have an extensive crystal collection to be successful. The truth is that having just one crystal is a great starting point, and it can help you figure out the direction that you'd like to go in next. It's better to buy your crystals slowly, anyway, because then, you will have time to dedicate to each stone that you bring into your home. A connection with crystals is paramount, as you will learn more about throughout this chapter.

If you can find a Wiccan or New Age store, you will be able to easily find the crystals and the other supplies that you may need. There are also sometimes stores that specifically sell crystals, but don't worry. If you don't have a shop nearby, there are several online stores that you can easily find. I prefer to show in person because then you can better feel what crystals you feel drawn to, but with some time and effort, you can work with any crystal that you have and build a connection with the crystals. The most important part is getting a crystal to start magic with and then building the connection with it because that's how you will benefit most from crystal magic.

You don't need to stress yourself out over obtaining crystals. There are plenty of avenues that you can take to find them, and you can determine what feels best for you in the process. You don't need to dive in 110% right away. Ease yourself into buying crystals and respond to what feels right. Let it happen as organically as possible because the better energies that you put into obtaining your crystals, the better you get out in my experience. When in doubt, let your instincts guide you. Try to get in touch with yourself, the Earth, and the divine to find the right crystals for you. Also, look for crystals that will best solve the predominant trouble areas of your life and then expand from there. Alternatively, focus on the crystals that are most predominantly used and paired with other crystals. You'll do just fine if you keep calm.

Tips for the Overwhelmed

So, I've given you an overview of how to get going on purchasing crystals, but many of you still probably feel overwhelmed. You're probably thinking, "Okay, but how do I even know where to start?" My suggestion is to start with a web search. Even if you plan on going to an in-person store, it can help prevent you from being overwhelmed if you have an idea of what options you'll have when you get to the store. You can start to look over prices and shapes to see what appeals to you. Just a little research can go a long way in making you feel more self-assured about your purchases.

Before you even look for crystals, you can cast a spell to ensure that you find good crystals in your search. You can formulate your intentions and speak what you want into existence. You may supplement your intentions by lighting a candle as you repeat what you want. Alternatively, you could make herbal potions that bring good luck and help you become more aligned with the Earth and the divine. Whatever magic you choose to do can help you create a balance that allows a better shopping experience as you choose crystals for the first time.

When you are shopping in person, feel free to stop thinking and instead let the magic happen. See what crystals you feel connected to, and if you can, put them in your dominant hand, and see how you feel when you are holding that crystal. Breathe in and let the energy of that crystal into your body. See how your physical and emotional selves respond to the crystal. Don't overthink it. Just use your feelings to determine whether that feels right. If you're shopping online, you won't have the same information to identify if the crystal feels right to you, but you can still try to look at the pictures and see what reactions they cause in you. Do your best to gauge your response to the crystals, but you can only do as much you can, so don't worry too much when you're shopping.

You're probably tabulating the money in your bank account, wondering how far that money, or lack thereof, will go. When you start to shop, there will be even more options than you dreamed there would be. Some of the crystals will come in lovely shapes, some will be raw, and some will be polished! The fancy pieces will be more expensive, so keep that in mind when you're planning on what you want to purchase and budgeting. Having a basic budget regarding how much you want to spend and on what can help you stay on track and focus your shopping. Also, keep in mind that how a crystal looks won't impact its magic. If you get something shaped nicely, it will work just the same as something that isn't, so if you don't have the budget, don't feel the need to buy the prettiest gems. If you do have the budget, by all means, buy whatever crystals call to you!

Look for smaller crystals when you are shopping. By looking for smaller crystals, you can save a lot of money, and you can save a lot of storage space too, if that is a concern of yours. Large gems can be great if you have space and money for them, but small ones can be so cost-effective, and they can easily be carried around as talismans if you are so inclined. Just like smoother stones don't work better than natural ones, bigger stones don't work better than smaller ones. The magic is in what you do with the crystals, not what the crystals look like, so don't get caught up in trying to get the biggest and most expensive things if doing so feels burdensome.

Don't buy everything all once. You need to be able to handle your crystals and put the energy required into using them. Buying so many crystals at once, not only is expensive, but it can be hard for you to pay attention to the crystals as they need. It's better to start with one or just a few so that until you get used to working with stones, you can direct your full attention to them to ensure that you are successfully incorporating them into your life. Magic isn't a race. You don't need to do everything right away. Work at a pace that makes you feel comfortable because it's better to do good quality work than a higher quantity of work when it comes to magic. You need to build a bond with your stones. It's kind of like a relationship, so imagine trying to make fifteen friends all at once! That's a lot harder than making fifteen friends one by one.

You don't have to buy anything new if you don't want to. However, new crystals are easier to find. You can obtain crystals in a myriad of ways. You might find secondhand crystals, or you may even find some yourself. Alternatively, some may be given as gifts. Accept the crystals as they come your way. Sometimes, some of the best crystals are the ones that you weren't looking for. They are the ones that unexpectedly come into your life and make you feel drawn to them organically. That feeling is one of the best that a Wiccan can feel. Sometimes, you just know. Don't fight that feeling.

It's okay to be a little stressed at first. I want you to stay as calm as possible, but if these new things make you feel a bit anxious, that's acceptable. You don't need to try to ignore the concerns you have. Instead, try to embrace them and work through them because by doing that, you will be in a better headspace to deal with the magic you are creating. Know that nothing happens overnight. It will take a while before you are fully incorporated into the Wiccan world, and even when you are, you'll still have learning to do. You will never stop learning, and that's part of the fulfillment of Wicca.

Let yourself make mistakes. You're not going to get everything perfect, so don't try. Let yourself try your best and be open to the mistakes you make. When you make mistakes, learn from them. You might buy one crystal and realize that you would rather another style. That's okay. You can still appreciate the crystal you have and save up to get the one that really appeals to you. No matter what you do, you will make mistakes, but don't let those mistakes force you into quitting something that is so rewarding when you exert the required energy.

When crystals come your way, be sure to be grateful and give thanks to your deities for their role in locating your crystals. Remember that the crystals are yours to have and that you are going to form a special connection with them. Embrace that connection. Let it fill you and let it better your magic. Enjoy the crystals as new parts of your life, and let good energies surround you. The crystals will bring good things if you believe in their power and harness it. Sometimes, you may want to give your old crystals to other people. When this happens, you may feel an intuitive sense that the crystals belong somewhere else. Alternatively, you may feel that they are drawn back to the Earth, and you can return them to the ground and let them be one with the Earth again.

Getting Acquainted with Your Crystals

It may seem silly to you, but you need to get to know your crystals. You have to listen to them and know what their wants are. You have to create a relationship with them, just like you would create a relationship with anything else in your life. The crystals all have unique energies. Even two crystals of the same kind can have incredibly different energies, so you have to pay attention to the energies of each crystal. Crystals need attention or they won't do anything for you! Let them become a part of your life rather than placing them aside and hoping that they will do something.

Before you try to use the energy of the crystal, I want you to hold it and take in its energies. Learn what it makes you feel and try to form a connection between it and you. It will serve you well to take some time to learn about your new crystals before you five into using them in spells. Before you do anything else, you should feel like you have a closeness to your crystals. Some crystals will connect with you more quickly than others. For example, I felt almost immediately connected to a stone given to me by my grandmother because of the emotional establishments already formed. You need to feel a level of closeness to all your crystals so that they can work properly.

You probably don't want to wait before you start doing spells with your crystals, but being patient is an important part of Wiccan magic. You have to put the work in before you can get any reward. Magic is all about being attuned to your surroundings and the natural and spiritual parts of Earth. Accordingly, nothing worthwhile is going to happen if you don't let those crucial connections form. Having to form a bond with your crystals should feel like something meditative and rewarding rather than like a chore. If it feels like a chore, you're in the wrong mindset for magic. You need to address any negative mindset that you may have if you want to be successful.

Cleansing Your Crystals

When you get your crystals, you are going to have to cleanse them. Likely, they have been handled by several other people before you, which means that those crystals are polluted with bad or distracting energies that will detract from your magic. The different energies aren't likely to harm you, but you still want to get rid of them so that your own energy is entirely in the crystal, and there are no little hiccups in your magic. Purifying your crystals also helps you establish a connection to them because they become your vessels and are connected fully to you and your magic.

You can clean your stones in whatever way that you desire. The easiest way to do this is probably just to wash your stone with water while repeating a purity spell such as, "Clear away the tainted energy of the hands and hearts that touched this gem before me." Your spell, of course, doesn't have to rhyme. It doesn't have to sound pretty, but some people like to carefully craft their words because they feel more empowered that way. Spells can be whatever you make them, so make them yours and embrace them. When you use water, be careful with soft gems and simply put small amounts of water on them so that they don't get destroyed. Be aware of the needs of your crystals during this process.

Another way to cleanse a crystal is to simply hold it in your hand under moonlight, light a candle, and cast a spell. The combination of these three actions is the way that I have found best cleanses the crystals for me. I usually use the incantation, "Under this your moon, Goddess, I hold this piece of Earth tenderly, hoping that it will guide me through the hardships and wonders that I will face. As the wax melts, melt away the polluted energies from this stone I hold dearly, and let the dim moonlight be one with the flame, so I can charge this stone with my own tongue of energy." Again, you can use whatever spell feels useful to you. During the new and full moon are ideal for cleansing your crystals, but you can cleanse them anytime that you please.

There are other ways that you cleanse your crystals, such as using incense or burying your stones under dirt in your yard for a while to connect them to Earth. Whatever cleansing spell you can think of will work as long as your intentions are strong. Use whatever calls to you to cleanse your stones. Sometimes, you may feel the need to use several distinct methods to accomplish your goals. Every so often, you'll want to repeat the cleansing process because they need refreshing every so often because of negative energies that may pass through them or mishandling by other people. Continue to take care of your crystals as long as they are yours. Ensure that they are cleansed and ready for the spells that you would like to use them for by tending to the crystals as they require.

Crystals will lose their luster if you do not care for them. They will not be as strong if you aren't sure to tend to them, so be sure that you always keep them in top shape, just as you would your car or your home or anything else that you valued.

Charging Crystals

When you have magic tools, they require charging. Just like your phone or laptop needs charging before you can do any work with them, so do magical tools. Of course, the charging with magical tools is done in a very different way, but the point is that when you plan to use things for magic, you have to put energy inside of them so that you can channel that energy through your spell. Different Wiccans have various stances on how this energy works and the nuanced details, but it is universal that making sure things contain good energy is important.

Beyond just charging your stones for spells, it is good to charge them anyway because even without a spell, having them around can improve your life, and they can send and absorb energy without you even having to tell them to do so. Because they are entities that naturally contain energy, they are going to deal with energy whether you charge them or not. Still, when you charge your objects, you are controlling the energy that is inside of them, which is what gives you so much power.

Keep in mind that when you charge things, you'll want to charge them in ways that reflect that item's power. Crystals have different properties, and when you keep those properties in mind while charging your items, you can better dictate how those crystals will be used when it comes time to cast a spell. Rose quartz is not the same as jade, and you shouldn't treat it as such. Just like you wouldn't like to be treated like another human because you're different, crystals need to be treated with different attitudes when being charged as well.

To charge your crystals, you can go about it in several ways. You can use the moonlight or the sunlight to charge your crystals as you cleanse them. You can also use methods such as sprinkling them with herbs or ringing a bell around them. Like always, your intentions are the most critical part of your charging because it is from your own power that you are spreading energy to the crystals. You can also customize your charging method to what you plan to use the crystal for. For example, if you want to use it for psychic intuition, the moon is a good source because it is connected to spiritual and psychic parts of you. Alternatively, if you're looking for balance, you can use herbs or soil to charge your crystals.

Aim to charge your crystals right after you have cleansed them so that they have not yet absorbed other energies and remain pure. Generally, if you are using a crystal in a spell, you should charge it for what you are doing again, even if you have charged it before, so that your charge reflects your intentions. When you charge it in this case, you can hold it in your hand and imagine your magical energy going into the crystal and feel it becoming linked to you. When using a crystal for spells, charge them right before you begin the spell.

Charging crystals, or any other magical devices, is a crucial part of spellwork and witchcraft. You want to be sure that the right energies and intentions are going into your crystals so that you can get the best results. The more you practice charging your crystals, the easier it will get. You may feel a little lost right now, but it is one of those processes that is best learned through experience because it is so individual. It is hard to go wrong when you charge your item, so if you're following your intuition and doing what feels right for your purposes, you probably are doing just fine. If you're part of a coven, you will likely have a community that can help you. Otherwise, there are also several online forums you can join that can give you more personal insight.

Creating Crystal Magic

The following instructions will give you a starting point for your magic. You can create your own spell and magic as you get more advanced. Still, beginners often like to be told what to say, so here are some fundamental crystal and incantation combinations that you use to make positive changes in areas that you struggle with the most. You can use crystals for almost any problem that you have, and here are only a few examples of the combinations you can use.

Protection

If you are feeling unsafe and would like an easy spell for protection, you can use black tourmaline as an excellent crystal that provides stability and security.

Light a black candle*, which is known for being protective, and read the following incantation with the black tourmaline in your hand.

At times, the world feels so unsafe. I feel doom upon me, breathing down my neck and trying to inundate me, but I won't let the pains and torments catch me as I go through life the best I can and try to survive. God and Goddess, let this black tourmaline protect me, so I can serve the Earth in the ways that you intend, and I can feel secure in the life I have ahead.

When you have finished the incantation, blow the candle out, and then, you may place the gem somewhere unique to you or in a place that you feel needs the most protection.

*If you do not have a black candle, you can use a white candle because in Wicca tradition, because white contains all the colors, it can be swapped for anyone color if you need it to be.

Positivity

To be more positive, you can also use the combination of a black candle, which keeps negativity away and a crystal. Follow the same protocols as above, but swap out the crystal and the incantation. Use lapis lazuli for your crystal because it helps you acknowledge the positivity even when life doesn't go to plan. Further, you can use the following incantation.

Life does not always go the way I hope, but I want to take the goodness in because I feel it around. Let the hope rush through this crystal and into me. Let the positivity begin, so I don't have to continue to worry about all the things that I cannot control.

Guilt

Peridot can be used to help you relieve your guilt. It can help you remember to love yourself again.

I am free from the guilt because I have learned that I am human, and I can only strive to do the best that I can. Now, I am learning to harbor more positive energy.

Place the peridot in a potion of lavender (either from a plant of essential oils), and tea. Mix in the petals of a flower that you love for added potency and a touch of something that is important to you. Write the thing you are guilty of on a small piece of paper and put that into the mix as well.

As you mix the potion, repeat the incantation several times. You can remove the crystal from the potion. Alternatively, you can leave it in and keep the crystal in the potion for a while and let it serve as a reminder and magical item for a week or so.

Anxiety or Stress

If you are feeling anxious or stressed, using a combination of amethyst and rose, quartz can really improve your mental state and help you feel calm.

Take the gems in your hands, one in each hand, and begin an incantation.

These gems I carry with me will keep the worry from my mind, so the weight that's on my shoulders can flee my body and give me the chance to focus on better things that will help me achieve all that I want to make real.

Keep the gems close to you to ward off anxiety. If there's something specific that is bothering you, you can add that item into the incantation and call it by name.

Anger

If you are feeling like you are struggling to control your anger and have too much of it building up in your body, howlite is a great choice to help you reduce your anger. You can carry it with you to help yourself keep a level head in stressful situations that may make your anger kick into high gear.

Light a red candle, and let it burn as you begin your incantation.

With the light of this candle, I will use the howlite to channel my rage and let it burn swiftly before it can consume me.

Blow out the candle, and then continue the incantation, picking up the stone with your non-dominant hand.

Let all the anger be absorbed into this crystal. Take the rage I feel and let it melt to calmness. Let the calm be my guide going ahead. Let this crystal look out for me.

Love

If you are dealing with lost love, wanting to repair hurting love, or are looking to find love to break through your loneliness, this is the spell for you.

In this spell, you are going to use both a ruby and rose quartz. You should start by laying down. Place the ruby and the rose quartz over your chest. Then, repeat your incantation as many times as you need.

I have been hurt by love before, but I want to try to bring the love back to me. I want to feel it in my heart and let the joy of love fill my whole body. I am lonely now, staying on my own, but there is someone out there who can fill my heart in the painful spots where these love magnifying crystals rest. These gems will remind me to keep my heart open to the love that could find me.

Mental Illness

You can use crystals to help you deal with your mental illnesses. As you know, many crystals deal with stress and anxiety, and several others also have the power to help you control addiction, eating disorders, and OCD as well.

My mind is burdened by an ailment that I cannot control. I feel powerless to my behaviors, but I do not have to give in to the forces that try to destroy me. I can use my energy to build a new start and heal my broken parts— both physical and mental.

Hold a jasper crystal in your non-dominant hand, knowing that this crystal can help you because it takes excess energy and balances it. It absorbs all the bad energies, and it allows you to become lighter mentally as a result. This crystal will allow you to resist negative impulses that come with mental illness and help you make choices that will benefit you rather than relieve your mental pain only momentarily. You may struggle, but in the end, you will come out ahead. Repeat the incantation several times until you feel that you and the crystal are starting to become linked and that your energy is radiated into that crystal.

When you finish the incantation, place the crystal somewhere that is relevant to your mental illness. For example, if you have OCD and like to brush your teeth compulsively, place the crystal next to your toothbrush. Alternatively, you could carry the jasper with you to feel its energy as you go about your day. It is up to you to decide where your crystal would be most meaningful.

CHAPTER 6
Beyond What Glimmers

Wiccan crystal magic goes much beyond the glimmering qualities of crystals. There are so many wonderful things combined. While it is easy to look at beautiful crystals like jade or ruby and see how lovely they are, it is much harder to look beyond that beauty and realize all the work and dedication it takes to master crystals and have them work in your favor. You won't just be able to make them work without investing parts of yourself. You need to have faith and believe in your own skills and the power that is inherent in the natural world as well as the divine and spiritual worlds. There is magic all around you, but you need to embrace it. You need to be unafraid of it. You need to let it fuel your skills rather than ignoring it. Accept crystal magic for what it is, and you will have worlds of delight.

Crystal magic is also about the wonder and blessedness of the Wiccan religion. It is a way to celebrate the God, the Goddess, and the Earth that they grace with such blessings. If you would like to be a Wiccan, you have to carry your religious practices and beliefs through all that you do. All your magic must channel the divine and the wonders that the divine brings. Embrace and adore what you the universe has given you, for it is holy. Every part of this earth has an energy that you can use to learn to your advantage. These energies will help you grow spiritually, physically, and mentally. All you have to do is allow them to be part of you. Let them thrive. Let the Wiccan faith guide you and embrace you as you are because Wiccans are open to all the people who have been rejected and disempowered by the rest of the world.

Wiccan crystal magic also incorporates all the amazing facets of witchcraft in ways that inspire and motivate people. It is not just an aimless form of witchcraft that has no organization or no rules. It has parameters while still giving you ample room to explore and figure out you really are. It is a lifestyle that incorporates so many different elements. Crystals are not just rocks to the practitioners who use them. They are not only pieces of jewelry. They are tools that you can use to embrace witchcraft and empower Wiccans to do better work on this earth. Those tools are ones that you too can channel and let them make you part of something bigger than yourself.

It is a way of embracing the magic that people have within all along, and it can be used to celebrate through rites, rituals, festivals, and spells. It is a way of engaging with all the things that Wiccans hold dear. When you practice crystal magic, you are reaching new levels of yourself, but you are also able to be part of a community. You have people who can tell you how to be your best self. Those people can send you in the right direction. Even if you work in solitary, there is a community out there that will welcome you and that you can relate to. There are thousands of Wiccans, and in such an interconnected world, you are never alone. Don't be afraid to spread the magic or reach out to other Wiccans. Being part of a community is the way that magic continues to be shared and handed down through the generations.

You must learn how to use your power for good because that is what Wiccans strive to do. Do not try to use crystal magic for evil because that is not in the spirit of the Wiccan Rede. You need to use your magic in ways that help yourself and the people you love without hurting others in the process. Be merciful and compassionate to others just as you would want others to be to you. Magic requires a great deal of responsibility, but if you remain kind and loving, you won't have to worry about straying from good.

It takes practice and work to build your magical repertoire, but it is nothing that you cannot do. You have so much power in your body and all the things around you. You don't need crystals to do magic, but they are one of the best tools that a witch can ever have. They are beautiful, but they are also so powerful. They allow you to focus on specific tasks and better harness the power that you've had all along. Don't be afraid of crystal magic. It can't hurt you unless you hurt yourself.

Throughout the process, you will learn what makes crystals so unique. It is one thing for me to tell you the magical properties of crystals, but it is much more remarkable for you to experiment and realize the wonders by yourself. Undoubtedly, crystal magic is something that you learn through exploration and experimentation. The more you try, the more you will learn, and the more you will be able to do. When you start to discover crystal magic, you will unlock parts of yourself and the world that you didn't even realize existed. You'll realize that you are so much more than you ever imagined. Through faith and magic, you can find new parts of yourself that are begging for you to awaken via witchcraft. Don't fight the magic within you anymore. Let it be free. Pick up a crystal and let its energy become one with you.

CONCLUSION

You have made it through to the end of the book, and I appreciate that you have made it this far. Thank you so much for reading, and I hope that you have learned the wonders of Wiccan crystal witchcraft. Of course, what you do next is now up to you, but if you enjoyed this book, I urge you to continue to explore all things Wicca and crystal witchcraft because this is only a starting point for the wonders that you can do. Imagine all the amazing feats that you could accomplish if you stay on this path. Witchcraft and Wicca both require practice and time, but when you invest in them, you get so much more in return.

Now that you have finished learning the fundamentals, you now need to put what you have learned into practice. Start with a few of the spells that I have given you. Also, make some spells of your own! Fill up your book of shadows with explorations of your craft, and if you want, join a Wiccan coven to find a community of like minded people who want the same things that you do. Whatever you choose to do going forward, please consider utilizing witchcraft to lessen the issues of your life and to find inner peace.

If this book was at all helpful to you, please leave a review on Amazon. Hopefully, this book has given you the knowledge you need to understand better what Wiccan witchcraft is. Now, go out and buy your first crystal. (I know you want to!)

DESCRIPTION

Wicca Crystal Magic is a straightforward book that will teach you the fundamentals that you need to start becoming a Wiccan, as well as to start Wiccan crystal witchcraft. This book is ideal for people who have just begun Wicca or who want more profound insight into how to combine both Wicca and crystal magic. Even people who have some experience with Wicca and witchcraft can already benefit from the concise and understandable descriptions and spells provided in this book.

Many people automatically assume that the terms Wicca and witchcraft are synonymous, but that couldn't be further from the truth. Wiccan is a religion that uses witchcraft while anyone, religious or not, can use witchcraft. Wicca is so much more than witchcraft, just as witchcraft is so much more than Wicca. Combined, the two areas nicely merge the divine with the supernatural. They allow you to connect to the cosmic forces while still connecting to the Earthly ones and yourself.

This book will give you all you need to know to change your life in ways that you never expected. If you feel stagnated and aren't sure what your purpose is, you can begin to learn who you are through magic and witchcraft. There's no need to continue living life feeling undervalued or out of touch with the natural world. Embrace everything that is around you rather than trying to ignore all the things that could make you stronger. Let yourself grow and welcome the beautiful energies that surround each of us.

In this book, you will:

- Learn what Wicca is and about the history of Wicca
- Be taught the different types of Wicca and how Wicca is different from other forms of witchcraft
- Understand the thirteen principles of Wicca as well as the Wiccan Rede
- Learn about Wiccan rituals and rites as well as the eight major Wiccan festivals
- Receive comprehensive definitions for a myriad of Wiccan and witchcraft terms

- Know how to start creating magic using crystals
- Get easy to understand details about the different crystals Wiccans use and what they can do for you
- Discover Wiccan crystal spells that will help you begin crystal witchcraft
- Start to embrace all that it means to be a Wiccan crystal witch

By the time you have read this book, you will have all the information you need to begin creating real, powerful magic. You will have the knowledge you need to decide whether the Wiccan route is right for you. Using this information, you can unleash new parts of yourself that you've only dreamed of finding. You will be able to take charge of your life, and you will grow as a person— spiritually, mentally, and physically. Everyone dreams of being magical at least sometimes, and through *Wicca Crystal Magic,* you can embrace those dreams while feeling happier and healthier in the process. You'll find a connection to a higher power, which will enable you to be more than just another one of billions of people. You are unique, so let that uniqueness thrive.

www.ingramcontent.com/pod-product-compliance
Lightning Source LLC
Chambersburg PA
CBHW071503070526
44578CB00001B/427